Miniature Punchneedle Embroidery

Simple Techniques, Beautiful Projects

LINDA REPASKY

Martingale®
& COMPANY

Miniature Punchneedle Embroidery:
Simple Techniques, Beautiful Projects
© 2006 by Linda Repasky

That Patchwork Place® is an imprint of
Martingale & Company®.

Martingale & Company
20205 144th Avenue NE
Woodinville, WA 98072-8478 USA
www.martingale-pub.com

Credits

President: Nancy J. Martin
CEO: Daniel J. Martin
VP and General Manager: Tom Wierzbicki
Publisher: Jane Hamada
Editorial Director: Mary V. Green
Managing Editor: Tina Cook
Technical Editor: Karen Costello Soltys
Copy Editor: Liz McGehee
Design Director: Stan Green
Illustrator: Laurel Strand
Cover and Text Designer: Stan Green
Photographer: Brent Kane

Printed in China
11 10 09 08 07 06   8 7 6 5 4 3 2

Library of Congress Cataloging-in-Publication Data
Repasky, Linda.
    Miniature punchneedle embroidery : simple
techniques, beautiful projects / Linda Repasky
        p. cm.
    ISBN 1-56477-646-8
    1. Embroidery. 2. Punched work. I. Title.
    TT770.R45 2006
    746.44—dc22

                                2005018349

Mission Statement

Dedicated to providing quality products and
service to inspire creativity.

Acknowledgments

This book has been a labor of love, made possible only with the encouragement and support of many other people. From the enthusiastic students in my punching classes to my many rug-hooking teachers and friends, I have learned so much and have been inspired to no end.

My local hooking group cheerfully endured many nights of frenzied punching as I worked on models for the projects. Pat Cross planted the seeds for this book and stood by my side as I dove into putting pen to paper. Karen Soltys offered editorial insights that polished my words and turned a fledgling manuscript into the book that you now hold. And Linda Van Wyk graciously allowed us to photograph all the projects in her shop, the Speckled Hen, in Snohomish, Washington.

I am so grateful, too, to my mother, Janet, who consistently nurtured creativity through her quiet example, and to my sister, Marci, whose many talents have always been an inspiration. And most of all, to the love of my life, Kevin, thank you for always being at my side, through thick and thin, with patience and good humor.

Contents

The World of Punchneedle Embroidery

In today's high-tech, hurry-up world, where nearly every hour seems scheduled, many of us are longing to do some handwork and create something unique. We begin projects, only to find that they take so much longer than we'd expected, and they end up being put aside for lack of time. Who among us doesn't have a collection of unfinished pieces of handwork?

Yet as busy as we are, we still feel pulled toward expressing our creativity, to make something special with our hands. What we really need is something that can be picked up and set down without a lot of preparation or fuss, something that doesn't require counting stitches and slavishly following a pattern, something that we can easily take along with us on car trips and into waiting rooms.

It may be these very desires that have brought miniature punchneedle embroidery out of the history books and into our hands. This delightful centuries-old needle art creates stunningly beautiful pieces with a richness of texture and color that belie the fact that they can be created in only a few hours. Resembling miniaturized versions of traditional hooked rugs, these punched pieces have an appeal that few other forms of needlework can claim. Pins, appliqués, dollhouse rugs, and framed artwork are among the many finished pieces that can be created using only a punchneedle and a few inexpensive supplies. Once you learn the basic technique, there's no limit to the variety of designs you can create using the punchneedle.

Not only is miniature punchneedle embroidery beautiful, easy, and quick, but it's also freeing. Rather than tediously counting stitches, you simply fill in areas of a design with color. It's freeing, too, to work on a project that doesn't require a great deal of concentration. Do your punching and talk with your family, watch TV, or chat on the phone. Miniature punchneedle embroidery is also incredibly portable. With such diminutive equipment, it's easy to toss everything

you need into a bag and take your project along so it can be worked in spare moments. And it makes the perfect travel companion on family and business trips, since it's easy to pack all your supplies into a tiny corner of a suitcase. (If you're traveling on a plane, it'll have to go in your checked bag, however.)

Because of its simplicity, it's easy to learn how to use the punchneedle. Children as young as seven or eight years old can readily learn to punch (with appropriate precautions about the very sharp point of the needle). Young or old, newcomers to punching quickly learn to create lush loops and can complete their first project in a couple of hours. Even your tenuous first attempt at punching will likely produce a great-looking finished piece, since you'll quickly become comfortable with the basic technique.

This book covers everything you need to know about creating miniature punched pieces, step by step, from threading such a peculiar-looking tool to forming luscious little loops on your fabric. We'll also spend some time learning about finishing and framing your work, with an eye toward using archival methods that will preserve your creations. And you'll get a chance to put your newly learned skills to use on a number of projects that are based on American primitive folk art. At the end of the book, you'll find a resource section to help you find supplies that may not be available locally.

Just a word of caution: punching can be addictive! It's so simple and so rewarding that you may begin seeing potential punched pieces everywhere you look.

Getting Started: Tools and Supplies

Happily, miniature punchneedle embroidery requires relatively few supplies. In fact, there's a good chance that you already have on hand many of the things you'll need.

Here's the "must have" list for your first project:

- Punchneedle
- ¼ yard weaver's cloth for backing fabric (this is what you'll be punching into)
- 4" embroidery hoop
- Embroidery floss
- Small, sharp scissors
- Good lighting (try a full-spectrum bulb)
- Small plastic box with lid
- 4"-long adhesive-backed magnetic strip

Note what is not on the list—a magnifier. Believe it or not, you don't need 20/20 eyesight or magnification to do this tiny form of needlework. Much of what you'll be doing doesn't require great precision. Rather, you'll be punching outlines and then filling them in. Most people find that having good lighting is much more important than using any form of magnification.

How Punchneedles Work

Unlike most other forms of needlework, punchneedle embroidery creates a lush surface, which is raised above the base fabric on which it is worked. Only one stitch is used when embroidering with the miniature punchneedle. Each stitch creates a tiny loop of thread. The loops quickly multiply to create a solid, almost velvetlike surface.

The punchneedle itself is very simple—a hollow needle set into a handle. A piece of thread or floss runs inside the hollow handle and needle and is then threaded through the needle's eye. The needle is pushed through a foundation fabric to create loops.

Selecting a Punchneedle

Punchneedles come in a variety of sizes and styles. Many of the punchneedles that you might find at yard sales and antique shops are designed for thick yarns, which are used for making floor rugs. As you can imagine, these are too large for the kind of work you'll be doing.

Instead, you're going to use a much smaller version of punchneedle, which is generically referred to as a "Russian punchneedle." There are two distinct styles of these small punchneedles, and you can use either kind. One style typically has a long plastic handle and an adjustable spring mechanism so you can set the length of the loops to a few predetermined lengths. The other style has a metal handle and is adjusted manually to make loops the precise length that you'd like (see page 8). Needle choice is a matter of personal preference; for our discussion here, I'll refer to one style as the "plastic-handled" punchneedle, and the other style as the "metal-handled" punchneedle.

Plastic-Handled Punchneedle

This punchneedle offers an all-in-one approach. You can adjust the length of loops quickly and easily by turning a knob or by clicking a spring-loaded mechanism to one of the preset levels. The plastic handle is long, which some people find easier to grasp. On the other hand, the handle is also relatively thick, which some people find more difficult to hold comfortably. Some brands have a single needle, while others offer two or three different sizes of interchangeable needles that you can remove and insert at will to accommodate all sizes of floss and thread.

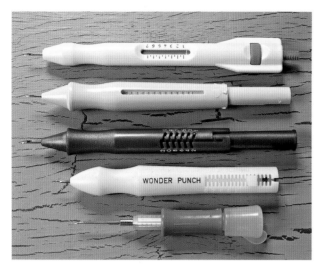

Some of today's plastic-handled punchneedles (top to bottom): Purr-fect Punch, Pretty Punch, Cameo Ultra-Punch, Wonder Punch, Clover Embroidery Stitching Tool

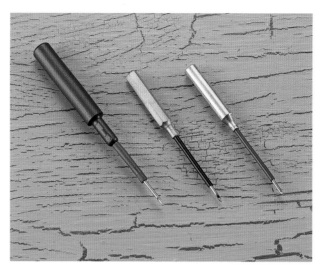

Three of the most popular metal-handled punchneedles (left to right): CTR, Bernadine's Russian Punch Needle, Igolochkoy Russian Punchneedle

Metal-Handled Punchneedle

Unlike the plastic-handled punchneedle, each metal-handled punchneedle has only one size of needle; the needles aren't interchangeable. To adjust the length of the loops, you cut a piece of plastic tubing (called a gauge) to make loops of the precise length you want. Additionally, the handles tend to be shorter and thinner than those of plastic-handled punchneedles. This type of punchneedle comes in three sizes:

One-strand. This is the finest, thinnest needle. You use only one strand of the six-stranded embroidery floss. It creates the most delicate and tiniest designs. Most plastic-handled punchneedles do not have a needle that is as fine as this.

Three-strand. This needle is a good, all-purpose size. You can use two or three strands of the six-stranded embroidery floss.

Six-strand. This is the largest of the Russian punchneedles. You can use four, five, or six strands of embroidery floss. This needle is used for larger, less-detailed designs.

With so many choices, you may be wondering which type of punchneedle to buy. As you've likely suspected, there is no single answer. There are pros and cons to both types. The metal-handled punchneedles tend to be more expensive, but they are popular because they allow you to precisely customize the length of your loops; many people feel that they give you greater control over your punching. The plastic-handled punchneedles cost less and will work well for many of your punching projects. However, they can be somewhat limiting, since they have predetermined settings for the length of your loops.

Many needlework and craft stores carry punchneedles, so check with your local shop. If you can't find what you're looking for locally, you can easily buy punchneedles by mail or via the Internet. See "Resources" on page 61 for a number of sources.

In this book, I'll be explaining punching based on using the metal-handled punchneedle. The projects in this book are designed for the three-strand punchneedle, so they are also suitable for plastic-handled needles.

Other Supplies You'll Need

Happily, you won't need to be very persnickety about the other supplies you'll be using, and you won't need

The basic supplies include weaver's cloth, an embroidery hoop, threads, and embroidery scissors or thread snips.

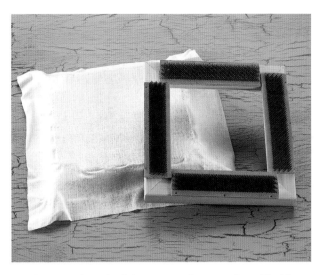

The fine metal teeth of the gripper frame grab and hold the fabric extremely taut, making a gripper frame a great alternative to a hoop.

to spend a fortune on them. Once you buy the punch-needle, the other supplies are relatively inexpensive. Following is the rundown on what we'll be using.

Woven Fabric

Using woven fabric for the backing of your punch-needle embroidery is critical, because it's the weave of the fabric that is going to hold your loops in place. If you're not sure whether a fabric is woven or not, look closely at the cloth. If you see threads crisscrossing at right angles, then you're holding a woven fabric. There are hundreds of options, but you'll want to use one that is somewhat tightly woven.

When you look at a fabric and don't see any threads at all, or if you see threads that have been knit to form a fabric (sweatshirts, for example), then these are not the woven fabrics you're looking for.

For your first projects, I recommend that you use weaver's cloth. This woven fabric is a blend of 45% cotton–55% polyester. You can buy it in nearly any fabric store, right off the bolt, at a very low cost. The polyester content helps make this fabric more resilient than purely cotton fabrics—and resiliency is what you'll want as you're learning to punch. Resiliency will allow

you to pull out loops that you're not satisfied with and then repunch into the same section of fabric. Using white or off-white fabric will make it easier to transfer your pattern and punch your design.

Embroidery Hoop or Frame

An embroidery hoop is critical for punching. If you've got an old wooden hoop tucked away in a drawer, leave it there! You need a hoop with an interlocking lip that will grip fabric and hold it drum-tight. The most readily available brand is the plastic Susan Bates Hoop-La, which is available in needlework shops, craft stores, and discount stores. Since our work will be small, you need only a 4" hoop to start.

For needleworkers who are serious about punching, there is another option called a gripper frame (shown above). Modeled after the frames used by rug hookers, this frame features carding strips that have thousands of tiny metal needles (or teeth), which grab the fabric and hang on to it. This frame is more expensive than the plastic hoop, but also does a far better job of holding the fabric taut. This frame is not manufactured commercially, but can be found through a few specialty online sources (see "Resources" on page 61).

Cotton Embroidery Floss

Rummage through your sewing basket and drawers, and you'll surely find some skeins of cotton embroidery floss, which is the standard for miniature punchneedle embroidery. New or old, any cotton embroidery floss that can be separated into six strands will work perfectly with your punchneedle. Nearly all floss has six strands, but note that the floss marketed as "craft floss" typically cannot be separated, so stay away from this.

Common brands of floss are DMC and Anchor, which are perfect for your first projects. In "Exploring Threads and Foundations" on page 23, we'll look at overdyed cotton floss as well as other types of threads and fibers, but for now, collect some skeins of ordinary cotton floss in colors you like.

Scissors

Use the smallest, sharpest embroidery scissors that you can get your hands on. You'll need scissors that are small and thin enough to clip the ends of the floss as close as possible to the backing fabric. The sharper and thinner the blades, the easier it will be for you to make clean cuts close to the fabric. Many people use curved embroidery scissors. Another option is metal spring-action snips, which provide a nice, close cut. I use Havel's Snip-Eze scissors (shown on page 9), which let me easily clip right at the surface of the fabric.

Adequate Lighting

Good lighting is essential to being a happy puncher. You don't need anything fancy. As long as you use a lamp that produces bright lighting, you'll be fine. It's nice to have a lamp that can be adjusted, so a simple, old-fashioned gooseneck desk lamp is great. I like to use a bulb that doesn't produce a lot of heat, so I use a full-spectrum bulb in my lamp rather than a halogen bulb. Full-spectrum lighting is especially helpful at night, when it's generally harder to see colors accurately. You can buy full-spectrum incandescent bulbs at the grocery or hardware store.

Miscellaneous Supplies

You will soon discover that punchneedles come with an essential tool—a threader. The threader is incredibly fine, made of wire that is as thin as a single strand of hair. The threader is not something you want to drop or you may never find it again. For that reason, I recommend that you buy a small plastic box to hold your punchneedle and supplies. Then attach a 4" length of adhesive-backed magnetic strip to the inside lid of the box. The magnet will do a great job of holding the threader with little risk of loss. Get into the habit of immediately placing the threader onto the magnet after every use.

A small box with a magnet adhered to the lid

GET A GRIP

Some punchneedles have very narrow brass or metal handles. If you find yourself wishing for a thicker handle, you can use a standard pencil grip for the CTR punchneedle. Other brands are too narrow for a pencil grip, so you'll need to improvise. Try using a high-density foam hair curler. Simply remove the inner metal rod and cut off a 1"-long piece. Slip this comfortably soft-yet-firm foam onto the thinnest of punchneedle handles for a great grip.

Make a cushioned grip from a foam hair curler.

Getting Ready: Prepping Your Floss and Fabric

Once you've gathered your basic supplies, you'll be eager to get started. But before you punch your first loop, you'll want to take a close look at this odd-looking tool and learn how to get it ready for punching.

Notice that the needle is hollow like a hypodermic needle and that the tip of the needle has an unusual point. Rather than gently angling to a point on all sides, the needle is cut sharply from one side to the other. When you punch, you will want to know which direction this beveled edge is facing; it plays a key role in creating good loops.

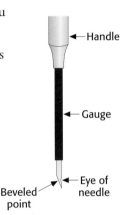

The "business" end of the punchneedle. Note the beveled point.

Also notice that your punchneedle has plastic tubing slipped over the needle. This is called the gauge. The gauge is what controls the length of your loops. Every time your needle pokes into the fabric, it's going to go as far as it can until that gauge hits the fabric. You can make the gauge longer or shorter to change the length of the loops.

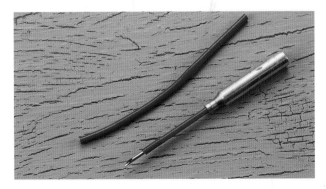

The Igolochkoy punchneedle with its red gauge

If you don't see any plastic tubing, it's likely that you have a plastic-handled punchneedle that is spring-loaded. Rather than using plastic tubing to stop the needle, this type of punchneedle simply uses the end of the handle to stop it. A spring mechanism or screwlike threads inside the handle make the needle shorter or longer and therefore adjust the length of your loops.

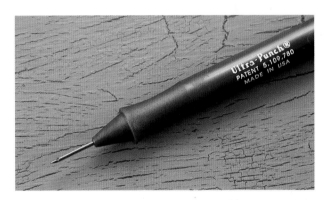

Note that the plastic-handled punchneedle does not have a plastic gauge.

Preparing the Backing Fabric

Cut an 8" square of weaver's cloth. If you can't find weaver's cloth, use a piece of muslin. Using a permanent felt-tipped marker, draw a few shapes onto the center of the fabric—some straight lines, a box, a curvy squiggle, a heart. You can draw these freehand, or use the pattern on the following page. These shapes will help you become accustomed to using the punchneedle and will also help you get a feel for the spacing of the loops, particularly for filling in large areas.

Use the practice pattern below to try your hand at punching straight lines and curves and at filling in closed spaces.

Practice pattern

Now you're ready to insert the fabric into the hoop. There is definitely a right way and a wrong way to do this, so follow these steps carefully.

1. Find the imprinted wording "this side up" on the edge of the inner (smaller) ring of the hoop. Set the inner ring down on a flat surface, with the wording facing up.

Make sure you can read "this side up" on the inner ring.

2. Place your fabric over the inner ring of the hoop, with the drawn shapes facing up. This is the side that you'll be working on. Your drawing is on the side that will become the back of the piece when you're done. The front side—the pretty loopy side—will be on the underside of the hoop as you're working.

3. Loosen the outer ring of the hoop quite a bit, place it on top of the fabric-covered inner ring, and push it down over the inner ring. Listen for a "click" as the outer hoop slides over the lip. You'll also feel the outer ring slip over the lip and settle in.

The hoop above has the fabric inserted correctly (note the raised surface of the fabric).

This hoop has the inner ring inserted upside down and thus will not hold the fabric well.

4. Use the screw on the hoop to tighten the outer ring. Slowly and gently, keep tightening the screw and tugging the fabric until the surface of the fabric is taut and square in the hoop. Very taut fabric is critical for making good loops.

Preparing the Floss for Punching

To find out how many strands of floss you'll need, check the instructions that accompany the pattern. Some projects require only one strand; others require two or sometimes three strands. In this book, the projects all use two strands of cotton embroidery floss or one strand of wool thread. For punching the shapes on the practice piece, use two strands of cotton embroidery floss in the three-strand punchneedle.

Here's a good way to work with the strands without creating a tangled mess. Pull a generous length of floss from the skein, about 30" to 36" long, and cut it. Grab the end of one of the six strands with your left hand, and hold the rest of the cut floss a few inches away with your right hand. Gently pull on the single strand with your left hand while maintaining a gentle grip on the remaining strands in your right hand. You'll see the one strand come out easily in your left hand, and the remaining strands will bunch up near the fingers of your right hand. As soon as you finish pulling out the one strand, the rest of the floss will unbunch itself.

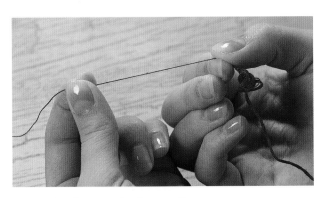

Separating the strands of cotton floss

Repeat this process for your second strand. Don't be tempted to take a shortcut by pulling out two or three strands at the same time unless you enjoy trying to untangle six strands of snarled floss.

Threading the Needle

Plastic- and metal-handled needles are threaded slightly differently. We'll cover the method used for the metal-handled punchneedles here. Plastic-handled punchneedles follow the same concept, but generally require a slightly different process. See the instructions that accompany your punchneedle.

Threading the needle may seem counterintuitive at first because you'll be working from the bottom of the needle, but after you've threaded your needle a few times, it becomes easy. First, get to know your threader. Notice that one end is folded with a twist, and the other end is joined or soldered. Each end plays an important role in the threading process.

Soldered end   Folded end

The threader

1. Hold the threader in your dominant hand. Hold the punchneedle in your other hand, with the tip of the needle facing your dominant hand.

2. Insert the looped end of the threader into the punchneedle, moving from the pointed end of the needle toward the handle. The soldered end of the threader should go through the needle last.

Insert the threader, folded end first.

3. Pull the threader through the top of the handle until about an inch or two of the threader pokes out. Don't pull the threader out all the way! Leave most of the threader inside the punchneedle.

4. Insert the floss into the looped tip of the threader so that 4" to 5" of floss is through the loop. Gently tug on the floss toward the fold in the threader, so that the fold can grip the floss and keep it in place as you continue.

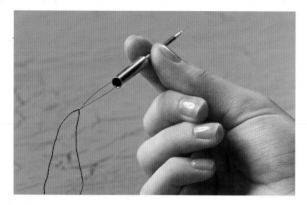

Slip one end of the floss into the threader, and give a slight tug to catch it in the fold.

5. Using your dominant hand, grab the soldered end of the threader (the end that's coming out of the tip of the needle) and pull the threader through the handle, and then completely out of the punch-needle. Pull about 8" of floss through the needle with the threader still attached.

Pull the threader from the soldered end until the folded end and floss are pulled out of the needle.

6. Insert the soldered end of the threader (the end that's not holding the floss) into the eye of the needle, moving from the hollow portion of the needle toward the outside of the needle.

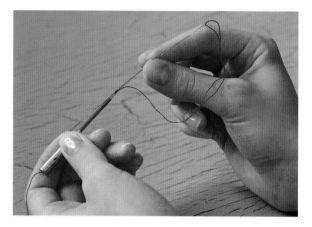

Thread the eye of the needle from the hollow inside toward the outside.

7. Pull the entire threader through the hole, along with several inches of floss. Release the floss from the wire threader, and voilà, you've threaded the punchneedle.

Pull the threader through the eye along with about 8" of floss.

Remember to put away the threader immediately! Slip it back into the tube that the punchneedle came in, or use the box with magnet described on page 10 to save yourself much frustration. The threading process is the trickiest part of learning to use the punchneedle. Pat yourself on the back, and know that the rest of punching will be a cakewalk.

Getting Loopy: The Punching Technique

You've threaded your needle. Your fabric is in the hoop. Get settled in a comfortable chair and you're ready to punch.

The Basics of Punching

Below is a short checklist of points to keep in mind while you're punching. Following this list are complete step-by-step directions for using your punchneedle.

- Work from right to left if you're right-handed or from left to right if you're left-handed.
- Keep the beveled side of the needle facing in the direction you're punching, and the tail of the floss trailing away in the opposite direction.
- Push the needle down as far as it will go each and every time.
- Barely lift the needle off the fabric as you finish a loop—just scrape across the fabric while you move the needle.

1. Hold the hoop in your nondominant hand. Don't punch onto a hoop that's lying flat on a table, because you can damage the point of the needle if it hits the table, and you'll also risk straining your neck.

2. Adjust the floss so that only about a 1"-long tail is coming out of the eye of the needle. You should have a long length of floss coming out of the top of the handle.

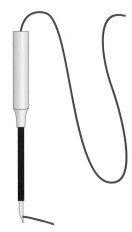

Only a short length of floss extends from the eye of the threaded punchneedle.

3. Hold the punchneedle in an upright position, at a 90° angle (perpendicular) to the fabric in the hoop as you punch. Try to avoid grasping the punchneedle as you would hold a pencil, since that would angle the punchneedle too deeply.

Hold the punchneedle upright.

4. Work from right to left if you are right-handed, and from left to right if you are left-handed. Hold the punchneedle so that the hollowed/angled side of the needle is facing the direction toward which you'll be punching. In other words, if you're right-handed, the angled edge of the needle should face left, and the 1" end of the floss will be trailing off to the right. Left-handers will have the angle facing right and the floss trailing to the left.

← Direction of punching

This side view shows the direction of punching. The beveled edge leads, and the tail of floss trails behind.

5. Insert the pointed end of the needle into the fabric and push the needle down as far as it will go. Every time you push the needle into the fabric, you will want to feel the fabric hit something solid (depending on the type of punchneedle you're using, this will be the gauge or the bottom of the handle). Punching the needle as far as it will go every time is the key to making sure that your loops will be an even height.

Note that the needle can go no farther, because the plastic gauge is stopping it.

6. When the needle has gone as far as it can, pull it up gently. You want the tip of the needle to just barely come back through the fabric; take care not to lift the needle far from the surface of the fabric. If you do, you'll discover that you've pulled out part or all of the previous loop.

After making a loop, pull the needle out of the fabric, but don't lift it away from the fabric surface.

7. Move the needle just a tiny bit to the left (or to the right if you're left-handed), scraping the surface of the fabric with the tip of the needle. Try to move it over only one or two threads in the fabric.

8. After moving the needle over, punch again, pushing the needle as far as it can go. Pull up so that the needle is just barely beyond the surface of the fabric, move the needle over a thread or two by scraping it along the surface of the fabric, and punch again. Repeat this process, punching slowly and steadily. Before long, you'll develop a rhythm, and punching will happen effortlessly.

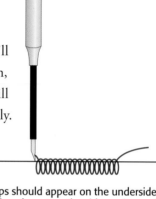

Loops should appear on the underside of your fabric only, not on the side you're working on.

CURVES AHEAD

As you punch curves, turn the hoop, rather than turning the needle. This helps keep the needle facing in the correct direction as you punch.

Ending the Floss

Continue making loops until you reach the end of your floss. You'll know the floss has run out when the needle makes empty holes in the fabric. You'll probably hear a difference in the sound of the punching, too. Simply lift the needle, rethread it, and start punching where the next stitch would have been.

The end of the floss you were using will likely leave a slightly longer tail on the loopy surface of your punching. You can go back later to fix this (see "Final Manicuring" on page 26).

When you need to change colors before you reach the end of your floss, use a fingertip on your non-punching hand to hold the floss at the base of the last loop you created. Press firmly onto the backing fabric to hold the floss in place and pull the needle several inches away from the fabric; then clip the floss as close as possible to the fabric before you move on.

Hold the floss tightly against the fabric as you pull the punchneedle away.

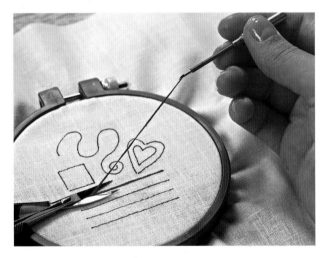

Clip the thread as close to the surface as you can.

Handy Punchneedle Pointers

- It's important to clip the tail of each new piece of floss after you've punched a few loops. A loose thread can easily be pulled or snagged, which could lead to accidentally pulling out all of your work.

- Try to rest the side of your hand that's holding the needle on the edge of the embroidery hoop. This helps provide some stability to your punching.

- Don't obstruct the flow of floss through the needle. It's all too easy to end up with the floss under your hand or arm, without even realizing it, and this can prevent the loops from forming evenly or from forming at all. To avoid this situation, lay the floss on top of your arm, from your wrist to your elbow.

- Keep your hand that's holding the hoop away from the underside of the fabric. The punchneedle is sharp!

- Try to avoid punching into previously punched loops. If this happens (and it surely will), the needle will push the existing loop into an elongated shape that will rise far above the other loops (see "Final Manicuring" on page 26 for how to fix this).

- Aim for a smooth surface on the back of your piece. If you're seeing bumps and loops on the back of your work (the side you're working on), it probably means that you're lifting the needle too high as it's coming out of the fabric. Your goal is to make the back of your piece very smooth—loops should appear only on the front side of your piece.

Aim for stitches that produce a flat, smooth surface on the back of your piece.

- Flip your work over often to check your progress and catch any problems sooner rather than later.

It's hard to know how the loops are looking on the front when you're working from the back.

- When you need to set aside your punching, there's no need to unthread your needle. Instead, just poke the needle down into the excess backing fabric at the side of the piece to park it. It will stay securely in place until you return to it.

Changing the Length of Your Loops

I usually have my gauge set at ¼", which is measured from the eye of the needle to the end of the gauge that hits the backing fabric. This creates short loops, which will be your mainstay. However, experiment to see what length loop you like best.

Adjusting the length of your loops varies based on the kind of punchneedle you're using. If you have a plastic-handled punchneedle, you can usually change the loop length by adjusting the spring mechanism to move the needle up or down. Try punching a number of loops to see if you like the new look of your loops and readjust if needed.

Many plastic-handled punchneedles use notches on the side of the handle to regulate the length of loops.

If you have a metal-handled punchneedle, adjust the loop length by changing the length of the plastic gauge. Your punchneedle comes with some extra plastic tubing. To make shorter loops, use a razor blade to cut the spare plastic tubing into very short pieces—about ¹⁄₁₆" long—and slip them onto the needle. (The gauge is so tiny that cutting it with scissors is awkward.) To make longer loops, slip off the gauge that came on the needle when you bought it, and cut a small piece off of it. When you put it back on the needle, it will make longer loops.

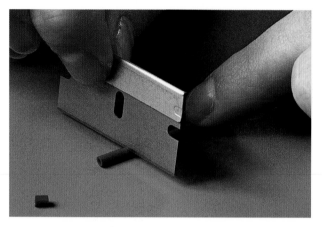

Use a razor blade and self-healing cutting mat to cut the plastic gauge to precisely the length you want.

You may want to make tiny adjustments even to short loops, to see what length most suits the piece that you're working on. Simply shorten the gauge by slipping off one of the short pieces you've added to the needle to make slightly longer loops. A word of caution: if your loops are too short, they may not stay in the fabric.

You can also create interesting effects with long loops. Leave them long and floppy, or clip the tops of the loops to give your work a plush, velvety appearance. You can even shape the loops as you clip them, to create a sculptured effect.

If you find that the small pieces of gauge slide around on the needle, hold a short piece of sewing thread beside the needle when you slip the gauge onto it. The added thickness of the thread will keep the gauge in place.

Don't throw away the cut lengths of gauge. Store them on a safety pin for the next time you need to adjust your gauge. And remember: longer gauge = shorter loops; shorter gauge = longer loops.

Punching Sequence

When you're punching a design, work from the center of your project toward the border. First, outline the portion of design you'll be working on. Then fill in with loops. You can follow the lines of the design as you fill it in, or you can punch in free-form, squiggly lines—do whatever feels most comfortable. Make your rows of punched loops about a needle width apart. Your individual stitches (loops) should be very close together, but the lines or rows of punched loops will be a bit farther apart. Be sure to completely fill in each area of your design. When you finish punching one motif in a design, move on to the next, outlining that motif and filling in, and continue to move out toward the borders.

Individual stitches form loops
that are very close together,
while the rows of loops
are spaced farther apart.

Punching truly straight lines can be tricky. You will likely find that it's easiest to punch straight lines by feel, following along a thread of the backing fabric, rather than drawing a line and trying to follow it. A drawn line can obscure the threads of the fabric, making it more difficult to punch in a straight line. Of course, if a few loops stray to either side of the line, it's likely that they won't even be noticed.

Punching the Background

Backgrounds are fun, because they give you plenty of opportunity to be creative. Before you work the background, punch a single line of loops around the outside border of your piece to keep the edges of your work nice and straight.

In addition, punch a single row of loops directly outside the outlines of all your motifs. Say, for example, that your design features a crow standing on a pumpkin. Before you fill in the background, use the background color to punch a line of loops all the way around these shapes, right beside the outlining loops.

This step helps your motifs keep their shape as you continue to punch.

After all motifs are outlined, you're ready to fill in the background. For any background, you can punch in rows that echo the shapes of your design until you reach the outer border of your piece. Or you could punch in random squiggles or swirls—a subtle way to create interest in the background.

Arrows show the direction
of punching on background.

MAKING MOTIFS STAND OUT

If your background color is close in color to any of your motifs, punch one or two rows of loops in a lighter or contrasting color around the motifs to help the shapes stand out. For instance, if you want your crow on a pumpkin to be in a night sky, the dark sky surrounding the crow would make the bird almost invisible. Punching a row or two of light gray or tan loops around the crow before you punch the sky will make him noticeable.

Backgrounds are also the perfect place to use over-dyed floss because their variations in color help create a subtle, mottled appearance that makes a piece more interesting to look at. See "Thread Choices for Punching" on page 23 for more information on overdyed floss. You can create a similar look by using two or more similar shades of solid floss. See page 24 for tips on blending floss colors.

If you're like most punchers, at first you'll think your punching looks awful and you'll wonder what you've done wrong. Most likely, you haven't done anything wrong at all. When you begin punching a design, you'll find that the loops are floppy and the design doesn't have much shape or definition. When you flip the hoop over to admire your work, all you'll see is a mishmash of loops leaning in every direction.

Don't worry. As you continue to fill in areas with more and more loops, the loops support one another and begin to stand upright. Before you know it, your loops begin looking like a design!

Every design looks messy when you first begin punching. The cat's eyes and nose appear to be a shapeless blob at first.

Once you fill in more loops, the design begins to take shape.

Fill in all of the background with loops so that you can't see any backing fabric showing through on the front side. It's a good idea to flip your hoop over to check on your work periodically so that you can catch any bare areas before you change floss colors.

Drawing Designs and Transferring Patterns

You can purchase kits with designs already marked on the fabric. However, to use any of the designs in this book, or when you want to create your own designs, you'll need to know how to get your design onto the backing fabric. Here are three relatively simple methods that you can use.

Method 1: Drawing Freehand

If you're one of those lucky souls who draws well enough to just put pen to fabric, grab a fine-point permanent marker and draw to your heart's content. Be sure to choose one (such as the Pigma Micron pen in size .05) that's designed to be used on fabric—other choices might bleed on the cloth.

NOTE: You'll need to reverse any lettering or numbers when you draw them on the backing fabric because you'll be punching from the wrong side.

Method 2: Using a Transfer Pen or Pencil

Happily, iron-on transfer pencils and pens are readily available for those of us who don't have the confidence to draw freehand. Use your transfer pen or pencil to trace your design on regular paper; then, following the directions that came with your pen or pencil, transfer the design to your backing fabric using your iron. This method automatically reverses your design, which is particularly handy if letters are involved.

Method 3: Using a Light Box

This is my favorite way to transfer a design. If you don't happen to have a light box lying around the house, you can buy one at a craft store. Or you can create a makeshift light box by placing a piece of glass or Plexiglas between two chairs and putting a light underneath. Some people use a glass coffee table as a light box by simply putting a lamp under the table.

Set the pattern on the glass and place your fabric over the pattern. The light underneath illuminates the pattern so that you can see it clearly through the fabric. Trace the design onto your square of cloth with a fine-point permanent marker and you're done. To use the patterns in this book, you may want to photocopy them first so that the patterns on the opposite side of the page don't show through. If you're including any words or numbers, remember to reverse them so that they read properly from the right side.

Drawing Straight Borderlines

You might think that this is the simplest part of transferring a design. Alas, I haven't found that to be so. Because it's so difficult to perfectly align the border of your drawn design with the threads in the backing fabric, you may want to skip drawing these outer lines when you're transferring the rest of your design. If you do draw them, you'll most likely end up with lines that aren't perfectly on the straight of the grain of the backing fabric.

An alternative is to simply mark each corner of the outside borders with a dot. Many people find that these dots are enough of a guide that they don't need to mark lines on the fabric to show the borders. In fact, my preference is to not draw lines, since they can obscure the weave of the fabric that guides me in punching a straight line.

If you prefer to have a drawn line to follow, use a hard-lead pencil with a sharp point and slip the point into the "groove" that's between two threads in the weave of the fabric. Run the point of your pencil in this groove from one corner to the next. If you hold the fabric tightly at the side nearest the starting point, the tautness of the fabric will help your pencil stay in that groove. Repeat this at each corner until you've got the entire outside border drawn.

GOING WITH THE GRAIN

Regardless of how you transfer the design onto the backing fabric, try to get it on the straight of the grain. If you draw your design on the diagonal (the bias), your work will likely look distorted because the fabric stretches most in this direction. Working on the straight of grain will also help your design keep its shape when you punch the border around it.

Dealing with Mistakes

Maybe you've accidentally caught the floss under your hand and pulled out loops. Or, the loops are too short or nonexistent in a section of your work. Or, perhaps you don't like a color you're using and want to replace it with something better. Whatever the situation, it's a simple matter to pull out the loops you don't like and repunch them.

To pull out loops, be sure that you're aiming for precisely the area that you want to remove. To remove an area that you've just punched—which means that the floss is still attached to your needle—simply grab the floss near the backing fabric and pull until you've undone the loops you don't like and then clip the floss. If you need to remove loops in an area you punched earlier and there's no tail of floss to grab with your fingers, use the tip of your needle to gently pull up the floss from the back side of your piece. These stitches will be tiny, so it may take a little effort to reach under them. Once you've loosened the floss with your needle, you can gently pull on the floss until all the offending loops have been removed. Clip the ends of the floss close to the fabric and throw away this piece of floss.

Before repunching in areas where you've removed loops, gently scrape your fingernail back and forth across the fabric to restore the fabric to its original weave. Then punch again. Weaver's cloth is particularly forgiving and allows you to repeatedly remove floss and punch in the same area without damaging the fabric.

TROUBLESHOOTING POINTERS FOR WHEN THINGS GO WRONG

It won't take long at all for you to become comfortable with the punchneedle. In the beginning, though, you might find that things aren't working as smoothly as you'd like. Here are solutions to some common problems.

What's Wrong	→ Try This
My loops won't stay in; they keep pulling out.	• Move the needle from one stitch to the next with the very tiniest of movements. • When you finish punching one loop and are ready to move to the next one, take care not to lift the needle into the air. Try to slide it along the surface of the fabric. • Remember that your needle should be moving from right to left if you're right-handed and from left to right if you're left-handed. • Is your fabric drum-tight? Make it as taut as you can. • Make sure that the floss isn't getting caught under your wrist or arm, and that it's not too thick for your needle. • Double-check to make sure that you've threaded the floss not just through the handle, but also through the hole in the needle. • Are your loops long enough to stay in the fabric? If not, make your loops longer by shortening the gauge. • Make sure the needle isn't too big for the thread you're using. If the needle leaves too big a hole in the fabric, the loops won't stay in place.
My loops are uneven.	• Push the needle into the fabric as far as it will go, *every* time you punch. This should create loops that are the same height. • Make sure that you aren't unwittingly catching the loose thread under your hand. If there's any pressure at all on the floss, the tugging action will prevent even loops from forming.
My loops look floppy and shapeless.	• This happens at the start of every piece. The more stitches you make, the more support each loop will get from its neighbors, and before long, your loops will be standing up straight and tall, and your design will take shape.
I've repunched so many times that I think I've ripped the fabric backing.	• Maybe you haven't really torn the fabric. Punching can loosen the weave, so you may be able to scratch the surface with your fingernail and bring it back into shape. • If the fabric is torn, apply a small piece of woven, iron-on interfacing to the back side of your backing fabric and punch through that.

Exploring Threads and Foundations

Now that you have a good grasp of the punching technique, let's explore some of the other options for working with your punchneedle. Needleworkers are usually thrilled to learn that they can use many of the beautiful fibers they've been accumulating over the years. Below are some of the choices that are available, not only for threads, but also for backing fabrics.

Thread Choices for Punching

You have virtually unlimited options when it comes to threads for punching. What's critical in selecting a thread is to be sure that it will run through the needle smoothly, without catching. If the thread gets caught inside the needle or is too thick to flow smoothly, then you'll have a hard time making any loops. Using a thread with nubs probably isn't a good choice, since the "bumps" in the thread will likely snag in the needle. Remember to use the appropriate size of needle for the thread thickness. Using a very fine thread in a very large or wide needle won't work well, because the needle will leave a hole in the fabric that's too big to hold the loops in place.

Cotton embroidery floss is the most well-known and readily available choice. It's relatively inexpensive, plus it comes in more than 400 colors, so most likely you'll be able to find the precise hues that you're looking for.

Just a few of the many varieties of threads and flosses suitable for punching

Raid your floss stash from cross-stitch projects you never finished, buy some floss the next time you visit a needlework or craft store, or watch for it at yard sales. Anchor and DMC are well-known brands of cotton embroidery floss, but any kind of cotton embroidery floss can be used as long as it can be separated—usually into six strands. The only kind of floss to avoid is "craft" floss, which cannot be separated into strands.

Overdyed cotton embroidery floss is a newer product that has become extremely popular with needlework artists. Overdyed floss is simply ordinary embroidery floss that has been re-dyed in a way that creates variations in color and value, from gently mottled to dramatically varied. Some overdyed floss has several different colors within a skein, for example, moving from green to blue to purple, or even red to blue to white. Other overdyed floss is more subtle in its variations, using a single color in a range of values from medium to dark, for example. Punching with overdyed floss produces shading and variation, which creates more interest to the eye and gives movement to your piece. This floss is somewhat more expensive than solid-colored floss. The three largest manufacturers of overdyed cotton embroidery floss are The Gentle Art, Weeks Dye Works, and Needle Necessities (see "Threads and Flosses" on page 62). You may also find other brands locally or online, as more dyers are beginning to make and sell their own overdyed cotton floss. All of them work beautifully in the punchneedle, so experiment with their colors and see which you like best.

Wool thread can give your piece a really special look. It has a duller, softer look than cotton floss and also has a slight fuzziness. Wool threads are also a bit more expensive than cotton floss. Wool thread that is fine enough for the three-strand needle can be found at many needlework shops. DMC Medicis wool works perfectly in the three-strand needle, as does naturally dyed imported wool from Renaissance Dyeing. You can also find overdyed wool thread made by Needle Necessities to use with your three-strand needle. And don't overlook the wool-acrylic blends, including Madeira Burmilana and Aurifil Lana.

The cottons and wools described above are used most often, but they're not your only choices. Poke around your house—or in needlework and craft shops—to see what else might work. For example, a single length of size 8 pearl cotton will work in your three-strand needle, and creates a lovely effect. Fine crochet cotton and tatting cotton will work, too, although they come in a more limited number of colors. Flower thread works wonderfully in the three-strand needle, too. You can even use regular sewing thread, right off the spool in a one-strand needle.

Silk floss comes in a wonderful array of colors. Rayon floss is deliciously shiny when you punch with it. It's also a lot slipperier than many other fibers, which may make it a bit harder to work with. You might want to try using some of the metallic threads, either alone or together with another fiber, for some interesting effects. Don't feel limited by the options shown and described here, though. If you see a thread that looks interesting, it's worth trying in the punch-needle. If it flows through the needle and you like how it looks, then you're off and running.

Creating a Mottled Look with Solid Threads

Uneven coloring can add a lot of interest and movement to your work in subtle but effective ways. Over-dyed cotton and wool have considerable variations of color within a single skein and easily add a pleasantly mottled look to your punched work. But if you can't find them in the colors you want, there are other ways that you can achieve this effect.

One way is to punch alternating rows or adjacent areas with threads of similar, but slightly different colors or values, such as a row of beige next to a row of tan. (See "Crow in the Berries" on page 48.) Or use similar colors by two different manufacturers (tomato red from DMC and tomato red from Anchor). Each company has its own dye formulas, so it's unlikely that their colors would be precisely the same. Continue punching in an alternating pattern and you will quickly see a gently striated effect begin to appear.

You can also achieve a mottled look using different colors in similar values. By alternating rows or areas of dark colors—black, charcoal gray, and dark purple—you can make a rich night sky with real depth and subtle movement. The background will look more interesting than if you had used a solid block of pure black.

Using Two Colors Simultaneously

Another way to create visual texture in your work is by using two or more colors in your needle at the same time. When you punch with two similar colors together, the result is usually a bit more subtle than the mottled look of overdyed threads. However, if you punch with two highly contrasting colors blended in the needle, you can create a much more dramatic effect. As you fill in an area with your blended threads, you'll see a richness and depth that can't be matched by using a single solid color. Experiment with color combinations to see what kinds of results you can get.

Two similar values of gold blended in the needle create subtle shading, while two high-contrast values make more of a tweed effect.

Fabrics for Punching

As mentioned earlier, the best fabric for punchneedle work, regardless of your skill level, is weaver's cloth. Other woven fabrics will work well, too. Cotton fabrics such as muslin and flannel are good for punching. Linen and linen/cotton blends work nicely, too. But these natural-fiber fabrics have more of a tendency to

tear, particularly if you have to repunch your loops. Try to avoid extremely thin and fine fabrics, such as cotton lawn, because they are too delicate to stand up to punching.

TIPS FOR USING NONTRADITIONAL FABRICS

If you're determined to use a fabric that's got a loose weave—or no weave—you'll need to take an extra step before you can put it into the hoop and begin punching.

A loosely woven fabric, by itself, just won't be able to hold your loops. And knit fabric, such as T-shirt or sweatshirt fabric, is too stretchy to punch into on its own. You can overcome these problems by ironing a piece of woven interfacing to the back side of the fabric. Select a woven interfacing (one with threads that you can see) that is heat-fusible. Look for one that has a fairly tight weave so that it can do the work of holding the loops.

1. Cut a piece of interfacing that's about ½" smaller than the fabric you'll be working with. Transfer your design onto the nonfusible side of the interfacing.
2. Preheat your iron to the temperature recommended for the interfacing. Iron the interfacing onto your loosely woven or knit fabric, let it cool, and you're ready to punch.
3. You may need to shorten the gauge of your punchneedle to make longer loops since you'll now be punching through two layers of fabric. You may have to shorten the gauge even more for thicker fabrics, such as sweatshirt material.
4. If you can't fit the hoop onto the fabric—for instance, a thick sweatshirt—you might find it easier to punch into weaver's cloth and then appliqué the completed design onto the sweatshirt with fabric glue, fusible web, or thread.

Finishing Your Punched Piece

Whether you want to frame your finished piece or turn it into a piece of wearable art, you'll first need to finish the edges. In this chapter we'll learn how to fix bare spots and deal with any loose threads or thread tails, finish the fabric edges in three ways, and steam or press the piece to make sure it blocks flat and true.

Final Manicuring

Before you take your finished piece out of the hoop, you'll want to double-check it to make sure that you don't have any bare spots in your work. Take a close look at the loopy surface on the front of your piece for any areas where the backing fabric may be showing. Stick a straight pin into any area that needs a few more loops, and turn your work to the back. The pin will mark the precise area where you'll need to do a bit more punching. Thread your punchneedle with the appropriate color and fill in with more loops.

Once you've filled any gaps, turn over your piece to the front again and check for any thread ends or extra-long loops that may be poking above the surface of your work. You won't want to leave those strays in place. You can deal with them in one of two ways.

Trimming

Clip the longer threads and loops with your scissors or snips so that they're even with the other loops. This is quick and easy to do, but there's a downside, too. When you cut the threads, there will be a slight difference in color; the cut threads will appear to be darker, particularly with cotton floss. It's just a slight difference, and many people won't notice it, so if it doesn't bother you, clipping those offending strays is quick and easy.

Adjusting with a Crochet Hook

If you don't like the idea of having darker spots on your piece, use a tiny steel crochet hook (0.75mm) to pull the extra-long loops and loose ends to the back of your piece. Slip the tip of the crochet hook into the fabric from the back side, grab the errant thread or elongated loop with the hook, and gently pull it until it's even with the other loops or pull it completely back to the underside of your piece. You may need to gently wiggle the crochet hook to help it get back through the backing fabric. If you've pulled any threads completely through to the back side, snip them off right away with your scissors.

While you're looking at the back side, also check to see if you have any other loose threads. Snip them off as close as you can to the backing fabric so that they won't get caught by a needle or finger, which could result in a string of ripped-out loops.

Steaming or Pressing

To remove your punching from the hoop, loosen the nut on the outer hoop and slip out the piece. How does it look? The goal is to have a finished piece that lies fairly flat, without curling or cupping. If it's not perfectly flat, that's OK. Remember that you've put a lot of loops into a relatively small area. When you release the fabric from the hoop, it's no longer stretched tight, so the fibers relax and the weave tightens up, pulling all your loops along with it. That means that sometimes your piece will cup very gently.

If you've punched far too many loops, it's possible that you've overpacked them. This can easily happen if you've punched your rows too close together, and can cause severe curling of your piece. Steaming or pressing can help straighten it out and make it lie flat. But remember to leave a bit more space between rows on your next project.

To steam your piece, heat your iron to the cotton setting and set it on "steam." Place your punched work, loopy side up, on the ironing board. Hold your iron about an inch or two over the punched piece for 5 to 10 seconds. Then let the piece sit on the ironing board for several hours so that it can dry flat. This process works with most fibers. However, some metallic threads are made with plastic, so be careful steaming them so you don't melt the loops. Rayons and silks need to be treated with more care, too. You may want to test a strand of these types of threads with your iron before pressing or steaming the final punched piece. They require a cooler iron than cotton and wool fibers.

If your piece still cups or curls, you may want to press it. Find an old white towel that is still soft and squishy, and lay it on your ironing board. Then place your punched piece on the towel, with the loopy side *facedown*. Wet a small piece of white cotton fabric to use as a pressing cloth. Get it really wet and then wring it out enough so that it isn't dripping but it's a bit wetter than damp. Place the wet pressing cloth on the back of your piece and press with your iron. Simply hold your iron in place, without moving it, for five seconds or so. Then flip your piece over, rewet the pressing cloth, and repeat on the front side. Remove the pressing cloth, but leave your piece on the ironing board. Don't move it until it's completely dry.

If your piece seems to be curling a lot, in addition to pressing it, let it dry with some weight on it. Place a white paper towel on top of your punched piece, and then lay two or three books on top of that. Let your piece dry for 24 hours before you move it.

Finishing the Edges

We'll cover three different ways to finish your punched work. It's purely a personal choice as to which method you use. No matter which finishing method you use, each serves two important purposes: ensuring that the fabric backing doesn't fray and loosen, and preventing any of the light background fabric from showing around the edges of your finished piece.

The two quicker methods involve the use of an adhesive—we'll refer to these as the fold-and-glue method and the glue-and-cut method—while the archival method is slightly more involved and uses a needle and thread rather than glue. There are pros and cons to each of these approaches. Using glue is fast. You can apply the glue in just a few seconds. The downside is that, over time, the glue might stain or otherwise affect your work. The archival method preserves your work for generations to come, but it takes a little more time and effort.

Don't feel compelled to use only the archival method. There are going to be a lot of pieces you don't intend to be heirlooms, and you can guiltlessly decide to use glue on these. In fact, you may want to use glue on all your work. It's a perfectly good way to finish a piece. However, when you want to be sure that your punching won't be discolored or "eaten" over time by the chemicals in glue, use the archival method.

The Fold-and-Glue Method

This method works particularly well with all-cotton fabrics and for pieces with straight borders. If you've used a blend with a synthetic content, such as weaver's cloth, then it may be a little more challenging. The synthetic fibers resist staying folded, which in turn will make it hard for the glue to hold as it dries. If you find that this is a problem, use the archival or glue-and-cut method.

1. Cut away the excess fabric, leaving about ½" of fabric around each side of your punched piece.

2. Fold back the excess fabric right at the edge of your punching, starting with the corners. Fold the corners diagonally and then fold each of the four sides of your punched piece. You want each fold to be right up against the edge of the punched border, so that you can't see the white fabric at all when you look at the front of your work.

3. Firmly crease the folds, using your fingers or fingernails, so that the folds will somewhat hold in place.

4. Using fabric glue, squeeze a thin bead of glue diagonally across the underside of each folded corner. Simply lift up each corner so you can get the glue underneath. Refold the corners and gently press down. Don't use too much glue or it will seep through to the front of your piece.

5. Apply a thin bead of fabric glue to the underside of the folded-fabric edges. Spread the line of glue with a small paintbrush or your fingertip. Refold the fabric and press down gently to ensure that all edges adhere to the back of the piece. Here, too, you want to use only enough glue to hold the fabric, to prevent any excess glue from appearing on the front of your piece.

6. Lay the piece on a flat surface to dry for several hours. You can place a heavy book on top of it so that it will stay perfectly flat. Slip a piece of wax paper under and on top of your punching to protect your book and work surface from the glue.

The Glue-and-Cut Method

This is the method to use if your piece has curved edges. You'll be trimming all excess fabric away from your punched piece so you won't have to deal with the bulk of folding back curved edges.

1. Place your finished piece facedown on a piece of wax paper. Apply a thin bead of fabric glue all the way around the edges of the wrong side of the punched design. Use your finger to smear the glue into the threads of the excess fabric all the way around the design. The glue should cover about ¼" from the last row of loops. Spread it onto the last few rows of loops as well. Try to make a thin coating of glue on the backs of the outer loops—enough so that the adhesive will hold them in place snugly, but not so much that the glue seeps through from the back onto the front of your piece.

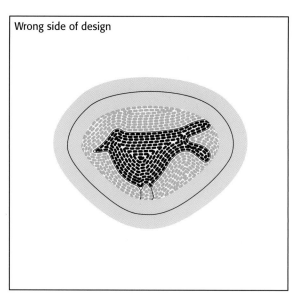

Wrong side of design

Gray area shows where to apply glue on the back of your piece.

2. Let the glue dry thoroughly. If you don't want to wait while nature takes its course, you can speed things up by using a hair dryer.

3. Once the glue is completely dry, cut off the excess backing fabric, using a pair of sharp scissors (but not your good fabric scissors). Trim as close as you can to the last row of loops, but go slowly to make sure that the blades of the scissors don't cut into any of the loops.

Trim the excess fabric away from the punching, cutting as close as possible to the outer row of loops.

The Archival Method

This method works on any fabric, but is easiest to use on pieces with straight outer edges. Curves can be tricky to manipulate. Begin by following steps 1–3 of the fold-and-glue method on page 27. Once you've folded and finger-pressed the excess fabric, you're ready to proceed.

1. Thread a hand-sewing needle with ordinary sewing thread. Any color is fine, since it won't be seen.

2. Working from the back of your piece, stitch the mitered folds at one corner to hold them in place. Take five or six stitches into the folded backing fabric only; you don't want to catch any of the punching with your sewing needle. Knot the thread so that it will stay in place, and clip it off. Don't worry about how your stitches look. They just need to hold the excess fabric firmly in place.

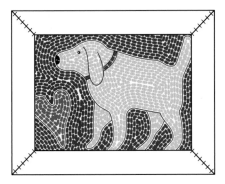

Stitch across the folded mitered corners.

3. Stitch the three remaining corners in the same manner.

Adding Twisted-Cord Edging

This decorative finish is optional. If you can't see the white of the backing fabric from the front or the side of your piece, you can skip this process. However, if you've used the glue-and-cut method, or if you can detect any folded backing fabric at the edges, then you'll want to make twisted cord and stitch it to your piece to hide the backing fabric. This is particularly important if the last row of punching is a dark color.

You wouldn't want its effect to be marred by white fabric peeking out around the edges.

Making a twisted cord is simple and gives a beautiful, polished edge to your work. The instructions may look long and complicated, but once you understand the concept, making cords is a cinch.

1. Measure the outside dimensions of your finished piece. If your punching is 2½" x 2", then you'll add together 2" + 2" + 2½" + 2½", for a total of 9". You'll need a piece of finished cord that is at least 9" long.

2. Cut two pieces of floss that are each four times as long as the length of finished cord you'll need. Continuing with our example, cut each piece 36" long (9" x 4 = 36").

SUBTLE OR BOLD EDGING?

You can use either two pieces of the same color floss or one piece each of two different colors for the twisted cord. For an edge that blends with your punched piece, use the same floss or thread you used in the outermost border of your piece. If you'd like a more prominent edging, use two contrasting colors. You can also adjust the thickness of your cording by increasing or decreasing the number of strands you use. Experiment!

3. Knot the two pieces of floss together at both ends. Slip one knotted end over a hook on the wall. I use a hook that's attached to a suction cup, something you can buy in any hardware store. I attach the suction cup to a window or a mirror and then remove it when I'm done.

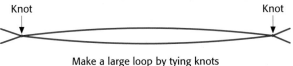

Knot   Knot

Make a large loop by tying knots
at each end of two lengths of floss.

4. Hold the other knotted end of the floss in your hand and begin twisting the cord. Most people

find it easiest to slip the loose end of the folded floss over their forefinger and draw little circles in the air, as if dialing a telephone.

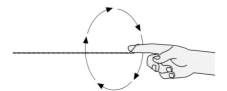

Twist the floss by using your finger to "dial" a phone. The floss will quickly twist.

5. Keep enough tension on the floss so that it stays taut as you twist. Every so often, stop twisting and slightly release the tension on the floss to see if it will twist onto itself. If it doesn't kink, then pull your hand back slightly to increase the tension and continue "dialing the phone" for more twists. You've twisted enough when the floss is eager to tightly twist upon itself when you loosen the tension.

6. Keeping the floss taut, put a finger at the half-way point on the length of floss and hold it there while you use your other hand to fold the floss in half. Bring the two knotted ends of floss together. Your finger should continue to hold tension at the midway point of the floss.

Fold the twisted cord in half, with one hand holding the midpoint taut, and hold both ends together at the hook.

7. Hold the two ends of floss together and remove your finger from the fold in the floss. As soon as you take your finger away, you'll see the floss wildly twisting upon itself. When the twisting stops, tie together the two knotted ends of floss, and the cord will stay twisted. For quick and easy twisting, you may want to try the Spinster, a gadget for making cord that can be found at needlework shops or on the Internet.

The finished cord

8. Lay the twisted cord at the edge of your punching, against the exposed edge of fabric at the side of your piece. Then, using sewing thread that matches the last row of punching or a single strand of matching embroidery floss, make small overcast stitches every ¼" or so to attach the cord. When you've sewn the cording all the way around, cut off any excess cord. Stitch five or six times over the cut end of the cord to make sure that it won't fray, and knot your thread to finish it off.

Framing and Other Display Options

Once the edges of your completed punched piece have been finished, you may want to take things a step further by framing it or making it into a pin. In this chapter, you'll gain an understanding of how to do both of these things.

Framing

Framing offers countless options. You can use a frame that has an opening the same size as your finished piece; however, many punched pieces are particularly attractive when they're placed in a somewhat larger frame. This way, they can be set off by a complementary mat, and the larger frame gives the artwork more of a presence. In this chapter, you'll learn how to frame your piece using an acid-free, archival method with fabric as your mat.

Supplies

- Purchased frame
- Fabric for mat
- Acid-free mat board
- Small, sharp craft knife (such as X-Acto)
- Needle and thread

Take your punched piece along when you go frame shopping, so that you can try it out at the store. You'll want a frame with proportions that will suit your work. In general, you'll find that a frame with massive, wide molding will overwhelm your diminutive work.

Selecting Fabric for the Mat

When it comes to selecting fabric for the mat, the options are staggering. You'll definitely want to have your needlework with you as you search for fabric, whether you rummage through your personal stash at home or head to the local fabric or quilt shop.

My best advice to you is to shop for fabric with an open mind. If you have a preconceived idea of what will work, you may not be able to find exactly what

you had in mind. Or if you do find it, it may not look nearly as good as you expected. Most likely, you'll know the right fabric for your piece when you see it.

Start with color. Do you want a light or dark mat? Are there any colors in the punched piece that you want to draw out by using a mat in that particular color? Do you want high contrast, so that your piece pops out at the viewer, or do you prefer low contrast, so that your piece melds gently into the mat?

Look at the size of the print. A large-scale print—life-size Hawaiian flowers, for example—would be difficult to use effectively. Smaller prints seem to work better. Another consideration is the busyness of the print. Is it so busy that it competes with your work? Then it's probably not the best choice. Prints with low-contrast colors might be the best option.

Consider what type of texture you'd like your mat to have. You'll have the widest variety of fabric selections in cotton. But what about using a soft, fuzzy wool? Or velvet? Silk has a subtle sheen that can give your piece extra richness. Even a coarsely woven fabric like burlap might give you precisely the look you want.

Select the fabric that you think will work best. Then set it aside for a few days and come back to look at it with fresh eyes. Do you still like it? Will it work? Then let's get started on the framing.

Preparing the Mat

1. Using a craft knife, cut a piece of acid-free mat board to fit inside the opening of your frame. Cut it just a smidgen smaller than the frame's opening to accommodate the thickness of the fabric you've

selected, because you'll be folding the fabric around the edges of the mat board.

2. Iron the fabric you've chosen for your mat, and cut it several inches longer and wider than the mat board. For example, if your mat board is 4" x 6", then cut your fabric 8" x 10". That will give you 2" of extra fabric on each side to wrap around the mat board.

3. Find the center of your fabric by folding it in half, first in one direction and then the other. The point where the folds intersect is the center of the fabric. Place your finished punched piece onto the fabric and center it. There's no need to measure. Simply "eyeball" the center of your punching and place it on the center of your fabric.

4. Thread a hand-sewing needle with sewing thread that matches the outside border and twisted cord on your piece. Hold the punched piece in place at the center of the fabric with one hand while you sew the needlework onto the fabric. You only need to catch a few threads at the corners to hold it in place. Try to avoid sewing into the punched area if you can; it's better to stitch into the piece's backing fabric so that you don't accidentally catch any of the loops.

5. Center your punched piece, which is now on the fabric, on the mat board. Lay a spare piece of mat board on top to keep everything in position and then flip the mat board over so you can work from the back. Fold the excess fabric around the edge of the mat board, mitering the corners as you do so. Stitch the corners enough to hold them in place, and then sew the excess fabric together by stitching back and forth across the back of the mat board in

a way that is similar to lacing a shoe. First sew the top and bottom fabric together and then sew the two sides together to hold the fabric firmly in place.

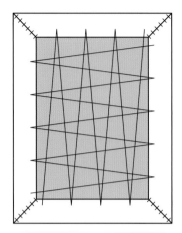

Fasten your piece onto mat board,
sewing from top to bottom and side to side.

6. Insert the mat into the frame, and you're done.

Making a Pin

Pins make great gifts. They're also wonderful conversation starters. When you wear one, people will undoubtedly be intrigued by this unusual form of needlework. Best of all, pins are easy to make. The "Crow Pin" on page 35 and "Portrait of a Sheep" on page 50 are both pins, but you could convert any of the projects into a pin if you like.

First, finish the edges of your piece, using any of the three methods described in "Finishing Your Punched Piece" on page 26. Because you'll need to use glue during the pin-making process, you might find it easier to use either of the glue methods rather than the sewing option for finishing the edges. Do not add twisted cord yet. That step will come later.

You'll need something to stiffen the punched work so that it can be worn as a pin without being floppy. I generally use quilter's template plastic. Pin backs can be found at most fabric and craft-supply stores or at online retailers.

Supplies

- Small piece of thin cardboard, plastic canvas, or heavyweight quilter's template plastic for stiffener
- Fabric glue
- Small piece of wool fabric or felt for pin backing
- 1¼" metal pin back
- Needle and thread

Assembling the Pin

1. Using all-purpose scissors, cut the stiffener so that it is roughly ¼" smaller all around than your punched piece.

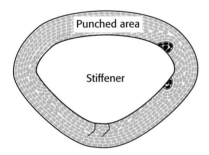

Be sure to cut the stiffener a bit smaller than your finished piece.

2. Spread fabric glue onto the underside of your pin-stiffener material, and center it on the back of your punched piece. Allow to dry.

3. While the glue is drying, cut a piece of felt or wool fabric 1" wider and longer than your pin. Choose a fabric color that complements the outer row of your punching for a professional-looking finished piece.

4. Center the pin back on the piece of felt or wool and sew it in place, stitching through the holes of the pin back several times to secure it. If you're right-handed, the clasp end of the pin back is ordinarily on your left as you're sewing.

5. Apply fabric glue to the stiffener that is already attached to your punching. Then carefully place the fabric pin back on the stiffener, so that you've got a sandwich of punching, stiffener, and felt or wool with the pin back. Center the pin back side to side, but position it a little higher than the vertical center so that the pin won't flop over when you wear it. Press the felt or wool into the glue for a firm hold and allow it to dry.

6. Cut away the excess felt or wool fabric, so that only a smidgen of it extends beyond the edge of your punching. By doing this, you create a very skinny "ledge" that will help support the twisted cord.

7. Make a twisted cord, referring to page 29, and lay it around the edge of your punching on the ledge of exposed felt or wool fabric. Sew the cording to the pin, using sewing thread or a single strand of matching floss. Use small overcast stitches every ¼" or so, making sure that your needle catches the fabric on the back and at the edge of the punching. When you've sewn all the way around your punched piece, snip off the extra cording and stitch over the cut cording several times to prevent fraying.

The Projects

There are endless design possibilities for punchneedle work. If you're not quite ready to draw your own patterns, then plunge into punching with any of the projects in this book. The patterns are designed to build and expand your skills, with the easiest projects appearing first and later projects becoming progressively more challenging. Remember, though, this isn't rocket science—even the most advanced project in this book is readily doable by anyone who has mastered the basics of punching.

Each project has detailed instructions, but feel free to do your own thing. After all, this is your project, and you should make it fit your preferences as well as the materials you can get your hands on. If the instructions call for wool thread and you can't find any, go ahead and use cotton. I used Anchor floss for my cotton projects, but if you want to punch with your stash of DMC, we've given the substitutions you'll need. (Conversion charts are available in needlework shops as well as online, too.) If you hate orange, substitute a color that you like better. Experiment! Sometimes the unlikeliest color combinations turn out to be spectacular. If you try something that you really don't like, just pull out the offending color and try another one.

And don't limit yourself to the designs in this book. Many needlework shops carry punchneedle embroidery patterns from a variety of artists, so check to see what's available. Even better, develop your own designs. You don't need to be a "real" artist to come up with patterns. In fact, simple drawings often make the most charming punched pieces.

What You'll Need for the Projects

Each of the projects in this chapter requires the following supplies:

- 8" square of weaver's cloth or other tightly woven foundation fabric
- Transfer pen or pencil and iron, or a light box (see page 20 for instructions on transferring the design onto your fabric)
- 4" hoop with interlocking lip
- Three-strand punchneedle
- Cotton floss or wool threads (see each project for specific color recommendations)

Thread Charts

The charts for cotton floss or wool thread that accompany each project refer to the following types of threads:

Anchor: Six-strand cotton embroidery floss in solid colors from Anchor

DMC: Six-strand cotton embroidery floss in solid colors from DMC

Gentle Art: Overdyed six-strand cotton embroidery floss from The Gentle Art

Weeks: Overdyed six-strand cotton embroidery floss from Weeks Dye Works

Medicis: Fine wool thread in solid colors from DMC

French Wool Overdyed: Overdyed fine wool thread from Needle Necessities

Crow Pin

This handsome pin is a great first project. It will give you a strong foundation in the basics of punching and prepare you for more challenging projects. You'll get comfortable with punching by learning to punch an outline and then filling it in with a single color. You'll also have a chance to see what happens when you blend two colors in the needle as you punch the background. As a bonus, this piece lets you make a free-form pin without having to worry about punching a truly straight line. Have fun with this little guy!

Finished Size: 2" x 1½"

Punching the Crow Pin

Use two strands of cotton floss throughout. See floss color chart on page 36.

1. Transfer the pattern on page 59 onto an 8" square of weaver's cloth, using one of the methods described on pages 20–21. Then insert the weaver's cloth into your embroidery hoop (see "Preparing the Backing Fabric" on page 11).
2. Using two strands of black floss, outline the crow. You can start anywhere, but punch the complete outline, including the beak.

ROTATE AS YOU GO

Remember to turn the hoop as you work around the bird, so that the beveled edge of the needle is always pointing in the direction you're punching. (If you're right-handed, you'll be punching from right to left.)

3. Fill in the body with more loops. Simply echo the shape of the crow's outline, row by row, to fill in

his body. Try to punch each successive row of loops about one needle width apart.

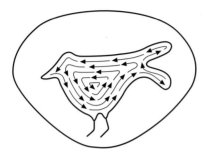

Arrows show the direction
of punching for motif.

COTTON EMBROIDERY FLOSS

The crow shown was punched using one skein of each Anchor color listed; DMC color substitutions are provided.

Used For	Color	Anchor	DMC
Crow	Black	403	310
Background	Light gold	1002	977
	Medium gold	1048	3776

4. Punch his legs with black floss. I punched only one row of loops for each leg, but if you prefer chubby legs, punch two rows of loops close together for each leg.

5. Thread the needle with one strand of light gold and one strand of medium gold. Using these two colors together will create a subtly blended look in the background. First, punch a single row of loops of gold all the way around the crow, including around each leg. Outlining the shapes first will help the crow keep his shape nicely. Then punch a single row of loops at the outside border of the background, using the same two gold colors. This row of punching will create the border of your pin and will keep the outside shape of the pin nice and smooth.

6. Fill in the background. You can punch in concentric rows around the shape of the crow, making ever-wider echoes until you reach the row of loops that forms the border. Because the lines of echo punching follow the shape of the crow, your background rows will reach the border sooner in some places than in others. Go back and fill in the empty areas with rows of loops that echo those smaller spaces.

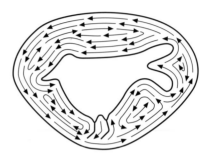

Direction of punching in
the background echoes the motif.

Finishing

1. Check your work before removing it from the hoop. Fill in any bare spots with loops and clip off stray threads.

2. See page 28 for details on finishing the edges of your piece and page 32 for instructions and supplies needed for turning the crow into a pin.

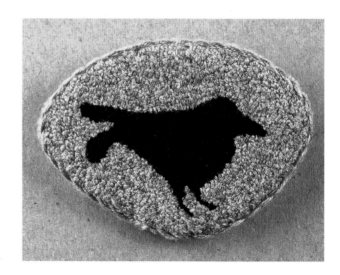

Antique Cat

Reminiscent of the cats that frequently appeared in very old, primitive hooked rugs, this kitty is simple and folksy, and his shape is a bit distorted. By using colors that appear somewhat faded and old, you will create an instant "antique." This project builds on your skills by encouraging you to use multiple solid colors in the cat to create the fur's texture. You're also introduced to a "manipulated" background that uses small squiggles of solid colors to create a surface with movement and interest. Overdyed threads can also be used for the cat and the background.

Finished Size: 1¾" x 2"

Punching the Antique Cat

Use two strands of cotton floss or one strand of wool thread throughout. See floss color chart on page 38.

1. Transfer the pattern on page 59 onto an 8" square of weaver's cloth, using one of the methods described on pages 20–21. Then insert the weaver's cloth into your embroidery hoop (see "Preparing the Backing Fabric" on page 11).

2. Punch the cat's eyes and nose using the dark brown floss or wool. Punch three or four loops, close together, for each eye. Similarly, punch three or four loops for the cat's nose.

SHAPELESS FACE?

The eyes and nose will initially look like shapeless blobs, so you might be tempted to pull them out and repunch them. Resist that temptation, since they will likely look perfectly fine when you later punch the rest of the face.

3. Using the medium blue floss or wool, punch the kitty's collar, making two rows of loops.

4. Using the cream floss or wool, punch a single row of loops to outline the light patch on the cat's chest. Then fill in this area with more loops.

5. Using the lightest brown floss or wool, outline the cat with a single row of loops. When outlining, you can either continue punching along the side edges of the collar—since many cats have fur that drapes over their collars—or you can stop punching just as you reach one edge of the collar and then start again on the other side.

6. Using the same light brown floss or wool, outline areas inside the cat. Punch a single row of loops around each eye and the nose to help give them shape. And punch a row of loops on both sides of the collar, as well as around the creamy patch on his chest.

7. Fill in the rest of the cat using all three colors of the light brown floss or wool. Create small, random blotches of the various light browns. Punch in curved lines that echo the shape of the cat until he is completely filled in with loops. Punch little squiggles, too, to create narrow areas of color.

8. For the background, use dark brown floss or wool and outline the cat with a single row of loops. Pay particular attention to the area between his legs and tail. The background needs to be distinct so that you can easily see the shape of each leg and the tail.

9. With the same floss or wool, punch a single row of loops at the outer border of the piece. Try to make this line as straight as possible, because these loops form the outer edge of your piece. Following along one of the threads in the backing fabric will help you punch in a straight line.

10. Fill in the rest of the background with random areas and squiggles of the dark brown flosses or wool thread. Punch in echo lines around the cat, or punch in small patches or chunks.

WOOL THREAD OR COTTON EMBROIDERY FLOSS

The cat shown was punched using one skein of each of the Medicis wool threads listed. Anchor and DMC colors are provided if you prefer to punch with cotton embroidery floss.

Used For	Color	Medicis	Anchor	DMC
Eyes and nose	Dark brown	8500	1088	838
Collar	Medium blue	8409	1068	3808
Cat's chest	Cream	8502	390	822
Cat's body*	Light brown	8611	1082	3864
		8503	1084	950
		8308	1080	3863
Background**	Dark brown	8500 (primary)	1088 (primary)	838 (primary)
		8306	360	898
		8309	1084	840
		8610	358	839

*If you're using cotton floss, instead of using a blend of the three solid colors for the cat's body, try using an overdyed floss: Cidermill Brown from Gentle Art or Mocha 1236 from Weeks.

**Likewise, try using two shades of either of the overdyed flosses for the background: Dark Chocolate and Maple Syrup from Gentle Art or Swamp Water 4129 and Molasses 1268 from Weeks.

WORKING WITH SOLID COLORS

If you are using solid-colored threads, use the lightest brown for outlining the cat. Then begin to fill in the cat, using the same light brown to fill in patches here and there. Switch to another light brown and do the same. Continue this way with the third light brown to give the finished cat a mottled look.

For the background, use the darkest of your browns to outline the cat and punch the border row. Then punch some squiggles in the background with the other browns. Fill in around the squiggles with the darkest brown.

Finishing

1. Check your work before removing it from the hoop. Fill in any bare spots with loops and clip off stray threads.
2. See page 27 for details on finishing the edges of your piece and page 31 for instructions and supplies needed for framing it.

Shelburne Goat

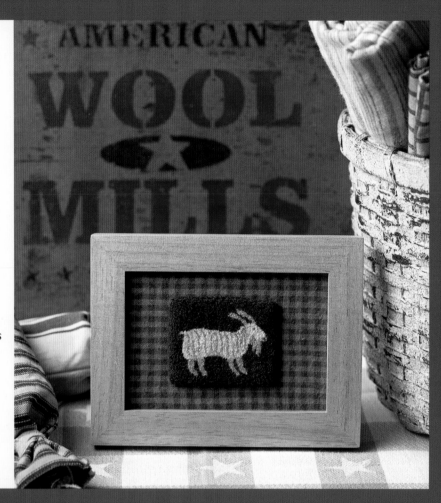

This goat was inspired by an antique butter mold at the Shelburne Museum in Shelburne, Vermont, which is a wonderful place filled with an amazing collection of American folk art. The squiggly lines in the goat will provide a good chance to practice your punching technique. It's a bit more challenging to keep the light-colored loops of the goat's body from intertwining with the darker lines because the lines are wavy.

Finished Size: 2¼" x 2"

Punching the Shelburne Goat

Use two strands of cotton floss or one strand of wool thread throughout. See floss color chart, opposite.

1. Transfer the pattern on page 59 onto an 8" square of weaver's cloth, using one of the methods described on pages 20–21. Then insert the weaver's cloth into your embroidery hoop (see "Preparing the Backing Fabric" on page 11).
2. Punch the vertical squiggly lines in the goat's body, using tan floss or wool. Punch a single row of loops for each line.

3. Punch the goat's nose and eye, using the brown floss or wool. Make only three or four loops for the eye and six or seven loops for the nose, because you won't want them to grow out of proportion to the rest of his face.
4. Use the cream floss or wool to punch a single row of loops to outline the goat's body and head. (Do not outline the beard, horn, or legs with cream.) Then outline around each of the tan vertical lines in his body, using the same cream floss. Punch a single row of loops around the goat's eye and around his nose. When all the cream outlining is

WOOL THREAD OR COTTON EMBROIDERY FLOSS

This piece was punched using one skein each of the Medicis wool thread listed. Anchor and DMC colors are provided if you prefer to punch with cotton embroidery floss.

Used For	Color	Medicis	Anchor	DMC
Beard, legs, horn, squiggly lines in body	Tan	8308	832	612
Eye and nose	Brown	8306	358	433
Head and body	Cream	8502	391	3033
Background*	Dark green	8404	862	895

*If you're using wool thread, you can substitute French Wool Overdyed 33 for the background color. If you're using cotton floss, instead of using a solid for the background, try Blue Spruce (Gentle Art) or Juniper 2158 (Weeks) overdyed cotton floss.

done, fill in the rest of his head and body with the cream thread.

5. Using the tan floss or wool, punch a single row of loops to outline the beard. Be sure to go all the way around, including under the chin where you've already punched in cream. Then fill in the rest of the beard with more tan loops. Repeat this process for each of his horns and legs, using the same tan thread.

6. Using the dark green floss or wool, punch a single row of loops all the way around the goat to create an outline. Then punch a single row of loops along the outer border of the piece. Strive to make this line as straight as possible, since it will be the outer edge of your work. Then simply punch throughout the background to fill it in.

Finishing

1. Check your work before removing it from the hoop. Fill in any bare spots with loops and clip off stray threads.

2. See page 27 for details on finishing the edges of your piece and page 31 for instructions and supplies needed for framing it.

Crockful of Posies

Old stoneware pottery and crocks are among the most familiar of early American household objects. A relatively easy project, this piece builds your skill in creating an interesting background through the use of overdyed and solid threads. In addition, the challenge of creating the thin stems, using a single line of loops, will build your confidence for more complex projects.

Finished Size: 2" x 2"

Punching the Crockful of Posies

Use two strands of cotton floss or one strand of wool thread throughout. See floss color chart, opposite.

1. Transfer the pattern on page 59 onto an 8" square of weaver's cloth, using one of the methods described on pages 20–21. Then insert the weaver's cloth into your embroidery hoop (see "Preparing the Backing Fabric" on page 11).

2. Because there are two colors along the edge of the crock, outline it in sections. Outline the deep blue areas first. Punch a single row of loops to outline the blue stripe in the lower portion of the pot. Fill in the area between the outlines with more blue. Using the same blue thread, outline the squiggly line on the top half of the pot, using a single line of loops. Then fill in between the blue outlines.

3. Using light brown floss or wool, outline the bottom section of the crock. Punch a single row along the bottom of the pot, up about ¼" along the side of the crock, across the crock just below the blue stripe, and back down the side. Fill in this

WOOL THREAD OR COTTON EMBROIDERY FLOSS

The crock of posies shown was punched using one skein of each of the Medicis and French Wool Overdyed threads. Anchor and DMC colors are provided if you prefer to punch with cotton embroidery floss; you will need one skein each of either the Anchor or DMC colors listed. Then use either the Gentle Art or Weeks overdyed flosses for the background and the crock.

Used For	Color	Medicis	French Wool Overdyed	Anchor	DMC	Gentle Art	Weeks
Lines on crock	Dark antique blue	8206		1036	3750		
Crock	Light brown		23			Cidermill Brown	Oak 1219
Stems and leaves	Light khaki green	8420		843	3012		
Flowers	Medium blue	8209		779	932		
Flowers	Gold	8303		363	436		
Flowers	Red	8106		1014	3830		
Background	Black		17			Black Crow	Mascara 3910

area with more loops. Next, punch an outline of the middle section, between the blue stripe and the squiggly blue line, and fill that in. Finally, punch an outline of the top section of the crock with more light brown loops and then fill that in.

4. Using the light khaki green floss or wool, punch the stems with a single row of loops. Outline each leaf and fill it in.

5. Outline the flowers and then fill them in, referring to the photograph for color placement.

6. Using the overdyed black cotton floss or wool, punch a single row of loops around the crock and around every stem, leaf, and flower. The stems are narrow, so take care not to get your black loops entangled between green loops.

7. Using the same floss or wool, punch a single row of loops along the outer border of the piece, following along a thread in the backing fabric to help you punch a straight line. To fill in the background, you can punch in lines that echo the crock and flowers, or punch in arbitrary lines and patches.

Finishing

1. Check your work before removing it from the hoop. Fill in any bare spots with loops and clip off stray threads.

2. See page 27 for details on finishing the edges of your piece and page 31 for instructions and supplies needed for framing it.

A Pooch with Heart

Our furry four-footed friends certainly find a way into our hearts. This slightly more challenging piece gives you the chance to really play with the background, since a single skein of the overdyed wool has several sumptuous colors that blend beautifully. The uneven colors of the wool used for the dog and the heart add to the richness of this piece.

Finished Size: 2¼" x 1¾"

Punching the Pooch with Heart

Use one strand of wool thread throughout. See color chart, opposite.

1. Transfer the pattern on page 59 onto an 8" square of weaver's cloth, using one of the methods described on pages 20–21. Then insert the weaver's cloth into your embroidery hoop (see "Preparing the Backing Fabric" on page 11).

2. Using red wool, outline the heart by punching a single row of loops. Then continue punching the interior of the heart by following the contours of the outline until it is completely filled in.

3. Using the black wool, punch the dog's eye with three closely spaced loops. Punch his nose by outlining and then filling it in.

4. Using the coffee brown wool, punch a single row of loops to outline the dog's ear. Use the same thread to punch a single row of loops to outline the dog's chest down to his front leg. (This will create a clear separation between the two front legs.) Similarly, outline the dog's belly by his hind legs. (Again, to create visual separation between the two legs.)

5. Using the dark blue green, punch the dog's collar. The collar will need only two, or at most, three rows of loops.

WOOL THREAD

The dog shown was punched using one skein of each of the solid and overdyed wool colors listed.

Used for	Color	Medicis	French Wool Overdyed
Heart	Variegated red		Voodoo Flame 55
Eye and nose	Black	Noir	
Outline of ear and legs	Coffee brown	8306	
Collar	Dark blue green	8409	
Dog body	Variegated tan		Driftwood 22
Inner border	Medium-dark garnet	8102	
Outer border	Ultradark delft blue	8200	
Background	Medium blue green	8407	
	Variegated blues and purples		Jewel of the Nile 83

6. Using the overdyed tan wool, outline the dog with one row of loops. Then punch a single row of loops around his eye, nose, ear, and collar. Also punch a row of loops against the brown outlines of the legs. Then fill in the rest of the dog with the tan wool.

7. Using the garnet wool, punch a single row of loops along the borderline drawn on the pattern.

8. Using the dark blue wool, punch two rows of loops just outside the garnet inner border.

9. To fill in the background, first punch two or three rows of loops around the dog's nose using the medium blue green. (This will help the nose to stand out and keep it from disappearing into the background.) Then punch several random patches of this color in the background. Switch to the overdyed blue/purple wool and punch a single row of loops to completely outline the dog and the heart. Also punch a single row of loops against the inner red border. Then continue filling in the background with the same wool. You can punch in curvy lines, in swirls, or in patches—the overdyed wool will create interesting effects of color as you punch.

Finishing

1. Check your work before removing it from the hoop. Fill in any bare spots with loops and clip off stray threads.

2. See page 27 for details on finishing the edges of your piece and page 31 for instructions and supplies needed for framing it.

Chicken Little

This chicken is surrounded by a border of colorful lamb's tongues—a decorative device frequently found on old hooked rugs and used with penny rugs and table mats as well. This is a great project for using the many odds and ends of floss you may already have at home—the more you have on hand, the richer the variety of colors you'll have for the border of this piece. Have fun selecting and punching a riot of color!

Finished Size: 2¼" x 1¾"

Punching Chicken Little

Use two strands of cotton floss throughout. See floss color chart, opposite.

1. Transfer the pattern on page 59 onto an 8" square of weaver's cloth, using one of the methods described on pages 20–21. Then insert the weaver's cloth into your embroidery hoop (see "Preparing the Backing Fabric" on page 11).
2. Using the light brown floss, punch the lines inside of the chicken's body and tail.
3. Use the black floss to punch three or four loops for the chicken's eye, keeping them very close together. While you still have black floss in the needle, punch a single row of loops along the outer borderline.
4. Using the beige floss, punch a single row of loops to outline the chicken's body. Punch all the way around the body, including her face, but don't outline the beak or comb.
5. Fill in her body with loops, using the same beige floss. First punch a single row of loops around the brown squiggles and lines you've already punched. Then punch around the eye and fill in the rest of the body, echoing the lines of the existing loops.
6. Using the orange floss, outline the beak, including the side where it adjoins the chicken's face. Then fill it in. Punch the comb in the same manner. Switch to the gold floss and punch one row of loops per leg.
7. For each lamb's tongue in the border, first punch the outside section—the one that will be against

COTTON EMBROIDERY FLOSS

The chicken shown was punched using one skein each of the Anchor solid and Gentle Art overdyed cotton floss colors. The DMC solid colors and Weeks overdyed colors are listed as alternatives.

Used For	Color	Anchor	DMC	Gentle Art	Weeks
Squiggles in chicken's body	Light brown	903	3790		
Eye and outside borderline	Black	403	310		
Chicken's body	Beige			Shaker White	Oak 1219
Beak and comb	Orange	323	722		
Legs and feet	Old gold	307	783		
Lamb's-tongue border	Variety of bright, medium, and light colors				
Background*	Black			Black Crow	Onyx 1304

*For a more interesting background, add occasional squiggles of other dark colors, such as Anchor 72, 150, 381, 403, 683, and 1041; or DMC 336, 938, 310, 500, and 844.

the dark background. Then continue punching, alternating colors, to fill in each lamb's tongue.

8. Using the black floss, punch a single row of loops around all the lamb's tongues to outline them. Also punch an outline row of loops around all parts of the chicken, including the legs. Fill in the rest of the background with black floss. For a more interesting background, punch occasional random squiggles using very dark shades of several colors, such as dark green, burgundy, purple, and dark brown, and fill in around them with black. These little bits of color add a slight sense of sparkle.

HAVE FUN WITH COLOR

For the lamb's-tongue border, select colors for the outer row of each lamb's tongue that are light or bright enough that they don't disappear into the background. You'll want enough contrast between the outer edge of the tongues and the background so that each tongue stands out.

Finishing

1. Check your work before removing it from the hoop. Fill in any bare spots with loops and clip off stray threads.

2. See page 27 for details on finishing the edges of your piece and page 31 for instructions and supplies needed for framing it.

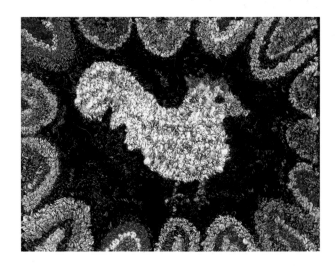

Crow in the Berries

Another crow! This time it's a bird with a bit more complexity. Use this project to experiment with creating a variegated effect without the use of any overdyed threads. By punching alternating rows of solid colors, the completed background is full of interest. You'll also gain experience in making tiny circles that retain their round shapes as you work on all those berries.

Finished Size: 2¾" x 1¾"

Punching the Crow in the Berries

Use one strand of wool thread or two strands of cotton floss throughout. See floss color chart, opposite.

1. Transfer the pattern on page 60 onto an 8" square of weaver's cloth, using one of the methods described on pages 20–21. Then insert the weaver's cloth into your embroidery hoop (see "Preparing the Backing Fabric" on page 11).

2. Using the taupe floss or wool, punch three or four loops for the crow's eye. Punch them very close together and avoid making too many loops. (You wouldn't want your crow to have a bulging eyeball, would you?)

3. Using the black floss or wool, punch a single row of loops to outline the crow. Punch two rows of loops, fairly close together, for each leg. Punch a single row of loops in a small circle around the taupe eye to help hold its shape. Then fill in the rest of the crow with black loops.

4. Still using black, punch a single row of loops all the way around the outside border of the piece, making these lines as straight as possible.

5. Using the light green floss or wool, punch some random curved lines in the grassy hill area for highlights.

6. Using the dark green floss or wool, outline the grassy hill on all four sides. Outline the light green

WOOL THREAD OR COTTON EMBROIDERY FLOSS

This piece was punched using one skein each of the solid-colored Medicis wool threads listed. Anchor and DMC colors are provided if you prefer to punch with cotton embroidery floss.

Used For	Color	Medicis	Anchor	DMC
Eye and background	Taupe	8505	831	613
Crow and outer border	Black	Noir	403	310
Grass	Light mossy green	8412	843	522
Grass, stems, and leaves	Dark mossy green	8417	269	937
Tree trunk and branches	Chocolate brown	8838	936	632
Berries	Red	8100	44	815
Inner ring of sun	Goldenrod	8026	305	725
Center ring of sun	Dark old gold	8324	309	781
Outer ring of sun	Olive gold	8304	907	3852
Background	Beige	8512	832	612

curved lines and then fill in the rest of the hill. Still using the dark green, punch the stem and leaves of the berry plant.

7. Outline the tree trunk and branches and then fill in the trunk, using the brown floss or wool.

8. Punch the berries on the tree and the plant, using the red floss or wool. Outline the berries first to define the round shape and then fill them in with more loops.

9. Using the three shades of gold, punch the sun in concentric rings as shown in the photo. Remember to outline each ring on all sides before filling in with loops.

10. Using the beige floss or wool, punch a single row of loops to outline around all the motifs. Punch completely around the tree and its branches and berries, the crow and the hill he's standing on, the berry plant, and the sun.

11. Switch to the taupe thread and punch a single echo line all the way around the motifs, right beside the beige outlining. When you finish with the taupe row, switch back to the beige thread

and punch yet another echo line. Continue alternating these colors until the background is completely filled in.

Finishing

1. Check your work before removing it from the hoop. Fill in any bare spots with loops and clip off stray threads.

2. See page 27 for details on finishing the edges of your piece and page 31 for instructions and supplies needed for framing it.

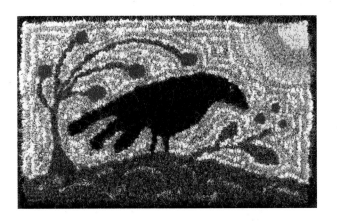

Portrait of a Sheep

This friendly sheep gets much of his character from wonderful overdyed wool threads. This project allows you to punch playfully with multivalued threads to create the sheep's rich and luscious wool and the grassy meadow behind him. You'll love watching the variations in color develop as you complete more and more of this project. The challenge here is in making the fine lines that outline his head and create his eyes and nose.

Size: 1½" x 2¼"

Punching the Portrait of a Sheep

Use one strand of wool thread throughout. See color chart, opposite.

1. Transfer the pattern on page 60 onto an 8" square of weaver's cloth, using one of the methods described on pages 20–21. Then insert the weaver's cloth into your embroidery hoop (see "Preparing the Backing Fabric" on page 11).

2. Using the dark taupe wool, punch a single row of loops to outline the side of the head and ear adjoining his body. This will ensure that the sheep's face doesn't get lost as you fill him in.

3. Using the dark teal wool, punch three or four loops very close together for each eye. Rethread the punchneedle with the medium brown wool, and punch the outline of his nose and a hint of a mouth.

4. Rather than outlining the entire sheep, work just on the head for now. Using the light-colored overdyed wool, punch a single row of loops along the side of the head and ear that will be against the grassy background. Once this is done, punch a single row of loops just inside the taupe outline on the other side of the head. Then outline each eye and the nose with a single row of loops. When the inner outlining

WOOL THREAD

The sheep shown was punched using one skein each of the solid and overdyed wool colors listed.

Used For	Color	Medicis	French Wool Overdyed
Outline of sheep's ear and head	Dark taupe	8839	
Eyes	Dark teal	8409	
Nose and mouth	Medium brown	8306	
Head and body	Shades of beiges		Driftwood 22
Background	Shades of greens		Meadow Green 32

is finished, fill in the rest of the sheep's head and ears, using the same color of wool.

5. Continue using the light-colored overdyed wool to outline the sheep's body. Punch across the sheep's back, alongside his head and ear, and down his chest. Continue punching a single row of loops along the curved portion of the border. Then fill in his body with more of the light-colored wool.

GOING IN CIRCLES

It's fun to see what effects you can achieve with the varied values and colors of the overdyed wool. For example, try punching lots of small spirals as you fill in the body. The sheep's wooly coat is the perfect place to experiment.

6. Using the green overdyed wool, punch a single row of loops along the curved outline of the border, beginning at the top of the sheep's back to the bottom of his chest. Take care to punch the outline with only the darker sections of the variegated wool thread. When you begin to make loops that are light yellow, stop punching and clip the thread. Pull a length of thread out of the needle until you reach a dark green portion, and resume punching. This will ensure that you have good contrast between the sheep and the background. There's no need to punch a green outline along the curved border where the sheep's body meets the border unless you prefer to have a green border all the way around the oval.

7. Fill in the rest of the green background. Just as with the sheep's body, you may want to experiment with a variety of different directions as you punch.

Finishing

1. Check your work before removing it from the hoop. Fill in any bare spots with loops and clip off stray threads.
2. See page 28 for details on finishing the edges of your piece and page 32 for instructions and supplies needed for turning the sheep into a pin.

Best Friends

Featuring a horse and dog amid hearts and bubbles, this piece is an adaptation of an antique quilt. It provides you with the opportunity to play with variations of color in the background. When I used the overdyed wool on this piece, I didn't care for all of the colors within a single skein, so I punched with only those sections of the thread that appealed to me. It's not hard to do, but it takes a bit of extra time with so much starting and stopping. This is a good example of how to manipulate threads.

Finished Size: 2" x 2½"

Punching Best Friends

Use two strands of cotton floss or one strand of wool thread throughout. See floss color chart, opposite.

1. Transfer the pattern on page 60 onto an 8" square of weaver's cloth, using one of the methods described on pages 20–21. Then insert the weaver's cloth into your embroidery hoop (see "Preparing the Backing Fabric" on page 11).

2. Using light brown floss or wool, punch three loops for the dog's eye and the horse's eye. Then outline the dog's ear and fill it in with the same color.

3. Using the reddish brown overdyed floss or wool, outline the dog with a single row of loops. Punch a row of loops very close around his eye so that the eye stays small. Also punch a row around his ear. Fill in the rest of the dog. Repeat this for the horse.

4. Using the dark red overdyed floss or wool, outline each heart and then fill in the hearts.

5. Punch the yellow, gold, teal, and red circles. As with the hearts, first punch a single row of loops to outline each circle before filling it in.

6. Using the overdyed green floss or wool, outline each motif in this piece—dog, horse, hearts, and

WOOL THREAD OR COTTON EMBROIDERY FLOSS

This piece was punched using one skein each of the Medicis and French Wool Overdyed threads listed. If you prefer to punch with cotton embroidery floss, use one skein each of either the Anchor or DMC solid colors and one skein each of either the Gentle Art or Weeks overdyed colors.

Used For	Color	Medicis	French Wool Overdyed	Anchor	DMC	Gentle Art	Weeks
Eyes and ear outline	Light brown	8308		1084	841		
Dog and horse	Reddish brown		25			Sarsaparilla	Rust 1326
Hearts	Dark red		53			Cherry Wine	Lancaster Red 1333
Circles	Yellow	8484		307	783		
	Gold	8302		1001	976		
	Teal	8416		851	3808		
	Red	8102		1006	304		
Background	Medium greens		39			Shutter Green	Kudzu 2200

circles—with a single row of loops. Using the same thread, punch a single row of loops to create the outside border, making the lines as straight as you can. Then fill in the background. Punch randomly or make echoing lines around the motifs.

Finishing

1. Check your work before removing it from the hoop. Fill in any bare spots with loops and clip off stray threads.
2. See page 27 for details on finishing the edges of your piece. This piece is attached to a piece of fabric in the same manner as described in "Framing" on page 31. However, rather than putting the matted piece in a frame, I put it in a painted wooden box (see page 62 for source).

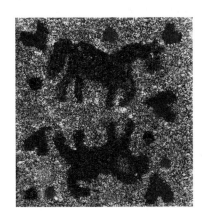

Tulip Cross

Thⁱs project is adapted from a much-beloved antique quilt block, the Tulip Cross. It is both beautiful and challenging, in great part because of its many small sections. Your well-honed threading skills will pay off with this project, since you'll need to change colors frequently. Using wool threads for this piece adds a subtlety and softness that best replicates the feel of an old quilt.

Finished Size: 2¼" x 2¼"

Punching the Tulip Cross

Use one strand of wool thread throughout. See color chart, opposite.

1. Transfer the pattern on page 60 onto an 8" square of weaver's cloth, using one of the methods described on pages 20–21. Then insert the weaver's cloth into your embroidery hoop (see "Preparing the Backing Fabric" on page 11).

2. Using the sky blue wool, punch four or five loops close together for the center of the flower in the center of the design.

3. Switch to the dark blue wool and punch a single row of outlining to define the middle section of the flower. Then punch more loops to fill in the area between the sky blue center and the outlining.

4. Using the sky blue wool, outline the outer edge of the center flower. Also punch a row along the inner edge of the outer section of the flower, right up against the dark blue loops. Fill in this area with sky blue loops.

5. Using one strand of the green wool, outline one of the large, long leaves and then fill it in. Repeat for

WOOL THREAD

The Tulip Cross was made using one skein each of the Medicis wool threads listed.

Used For	Color	Medicis
Center flower and borderline	Sky blue	8208
Middle section of center flower	Dark blue	8205
Stems and leaves	Mossy green	8411
Tulip bases, border tulips, and centers of small flowers	Rusty gold	8302
Tulip centers	Medium taupe	8840
Small flowers	Brighter gold	8325
Background	Black	Noir

the remaining three large leaves. Using the same wool, punch a single row of loops for one of the tulip stems and punch one or two rows of loops for each tiny leaf. Repeat for each of the other three stems with leaves.

6. Using the rusty gold wool, punch the outline of the base of each tulip—these are the flowers that point toward the corners—and then fill each one in. With the same wool, punch three or four loops for the center of each of the eight small flowers— these are the flowers that are on both sides of the tulips.

7. Using the taupe wool, outline and fill in the centers of the tulips in the four corners.

8. Using the brighter gold wool, outline the small flowers and then fill them in with the same color.

9. Using the rusty gold wool, punch the stylized tulips in the border. Punch an outline of each tulip and then fill it in. Repeat all the way around the border.

10. Switching back to the sky blue wool, punch the lines between the tulips in the border. You can use a single row of loops, or you can punch two rows of loops very close together to make your blue border stand out more.

11. Using the black wool, punch a single row of loops at the outer edge of the piece to create an outer border. Follow along a thread in the backing fabric to help keep your punching straight. Then outline every portion of the design with the black wool. Fill in the rest of the background, using the black wool. Make sure you've filled in all the miniscule gaps.

Finishing

1. Congratulations! You've finished a really challenging piece. Check your work before removing it from the hoop. Fill in any bare spots with loops and clip off stray threads.

2. See page 27 for details on finishing the edges of your piece and page 31 for directions and supplies needed for framing it.

The Trout

Fish provide us with the most amazing arrays of color. Trout in particular have wonderful patterns and hues. This trout gives you the opportunity to dabble with both subtle and extreme color shifts. Much like the "Best Friends" project on page 52, you'll need to manipulate the threads to achieve the color effects you want, since no one is yet producing the perfect skein of "trout." The challenge of this project is color!

Finished Size: 3⅜" x 1⅜"

Punching the Trout

Use two strands of cotton floss or one strand of wool thread throughout. See floss color chart, opposite.

1. Transfer the pattern on page 60 onto an 8" square of weaver's cloth, using one of the methods described on pages 20–21. Then insert the weaver's cloth into your embroidery hoop (see "Preparing the Backing Fabric" on page 11).

2. Outline the fish with a single row of black loops. Referring to the photograph on page 58, notice that the entire fish body is outlined, as well as the top and bottom fins. Still using the black floss or wool, punch three loops very close together for its eye. Punch the two curved gill lines behind the eye. Outline and fill in the small fin on the front portion of the lower belly. Finally, create all those little black spots. Outline each small spot and fill it in as you go. Each spot will take just a few loops.

NOTE: Don't be alarmed when you flip your piece over to take a peek at how it looks. Until the body of the fish is punched, the black loops will look like a sloppy mishmash. But don't rip them out. Wait to see how the spots look after you've filled in more of the fish.

WOOL THREAD OR COTTON EMBROIDERY FLOSS

The trout was punched using one skein each of the Medicis and French Wool Overdyed threads listed. If you prefer to punch with cotton embroidery floss, use one skein each of the Anchor or DMC solid colors and one skein each of either the Gentle Art or Weeks colors.

Used For	Color	Medicis	French Wool Overdyed	Anchor	DMC	Gentle Art	Weeks
Outline, eye, gills, spots, and border	Black	Noir		403	310		
Fish body	Green		32 Meadow Green			Shutter Green	Ivy 2198
Fish belly, fins, and tail	Variegated yellow/orange/red		43 Sedona Rust 79 Salsa 91 Sunfire			Fragrant Cloves, Harvest Moon	Fiesta 4131
Background	Variegated medium blue		13 Azure Blue			Morning Glory	Periwinkle 2337

3. Using the black floss or wool, punch the border outline and then punch another row just inside of the first row. Take care to make these lines as straight as possible.

4. Using the green overdyed floss or wool, punch a single row of loops inside the black outline on the top portion of the fish. Refer to the photograph to see which portions of the fish are green. To finish outlining the green portion of the fish, I opted to make a squiggly row of punching along the midsection of the fish. This gives a more natural-looking transition of colors on the belly.

NOTE: I manipulated the thread a bit, since I didn't care for the wide range of values in the wool I was using. See the "Use What You Like" box on page 53 for tips on thread manipulation.

5. Still using the overdyed green thread, punch around the eye, gills, and fin. Then punch around each of the fish's spots. Here, too, I continued to clip off those sections of thread that had the color I didn't want. Fill in the rest of the outlined portion of the fish's body.

6. The underbelly of the fish is where you'll have fun with the transitions of color, from green to yellow to rusty orange to red. Here, too, I was picky about the sections of wool thread that I used. Thread your needle with any of the overdyed threads for the belly and begin blending the colors and letting them gently shift into one another. The overdyed thread works very well for this, since the changes in color within the thread will help you create the effect you want. This is your fish, and he doesn't need to be realistic—use the sections of color that please you most.

7. Working with the overdyed threads, punch the three fins, gently transitioning from one color to another, using the colors you like best.

8. For the tail, I outlined portions with light yellow green sections of the overdyed thread, and other sections with darker greens. I used these same two colors as well as a section of the thread that contained some red to fill in the tail. You can follow the same color scheme or select colors that you feel will look best on your fish.

9. For the background, use the overdyed blue floss or wool to punch a single row of loops all the way around the outline of the fish. Next, punch a row of loops right up against the black border; then fill in the background. Try punching in swirls or squiggly lines to create the impression of water.

Finishing

1. Check your work before removing it from the hoop. Fill in any bare spots with loops and clip off stray threads.

2. See page 27 for details on finishing the edges of your piece.

3. This piece is attached to a small fabric pouch used to store crochet hooks. This pouch is equally handy for carrying your punchneedle supplies (see "Other Supplies" on page 62). Stitch the punched piece to the flap of the pouch as you would to a fabric mat when framing a piece (see page 31 for details).

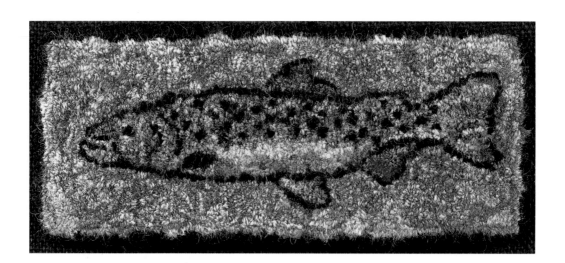

Punchneedle Patterns

All patterns are full size and are ready to transfer to your background fabric. They are the mirror image of the final punched design because you'll be working from the back of each piece.

Crow Pin

Antique Cat

Shelburne Goat

Crockful of Posies

A Pooch with Heart

Chicken Little

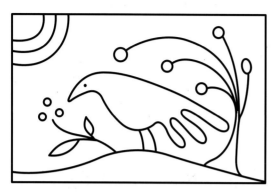

Crow in the Berries

Portrait of a Sheep

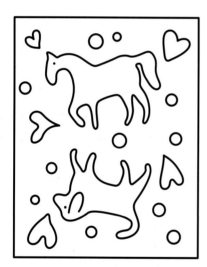

Best Friends

Tulip Cross

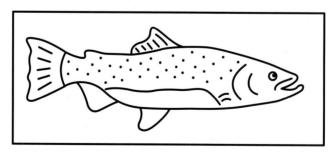

The Trout

Resources

Look for punchneedles in your local needlework shop. You can also purchase them online from a wide range of needlework retailers. One online store, www.punchneedlemarketplace.com, carries an extensive array of punchneedles. Below is information on the makers of some of the most popular punchneedles currently available. Sources for other punchneedle supplies can be found on the following pages.

Metal-Handled Punchneedles

Bernadine's Punch Needles
Bernadine's Needle Art
PO Box 287
Arthur, IL 61911
217-543-2996
Web site: www.bernadinesneedleart.com
Email: bernadines@consolidated.net

CTR Punch Needles
CTR Inc.
1334 Indian Creek Valley Rd.
PO Box 154
Melcroft, PA 15462
724-455-2111
Web site: www.ctrneedleworks.com
Email: info@ctrmachineandfab.com

Igolochkoy Russian Punchneedles
Birdhouse Enterprises
4438 G St.
Sacramento, CA 95819
916-452-5212
Web site: www.igolochkoy.com
Email: gail@gailbird.com

Plastic-Handled Punchneedles

Cameo Ultra-Punch
Distributed in the U.S. by:
Punch Needle Marketplace
Brohman's Inc.
333-335 Pam Dr.
Derrien Springs, MI 49103
1-800-272-1966
Web site: www.punchneedlemarketplace.com
Email: sales@punchneedlemarketplace.com

Clover Embroidery Stitching Tool
Clover Needlecraft Inc.
13438 Alondra Blvd.
Cerritos, CA 90703
Web site: www.clover-usa.com
Email: cni@clover-usa.com

Pretty Punch
710 West Broadway, Ste. 504
Mesa, AZ 85210
1-800-486-1234
Web site: www.prettypunch.com
Email: info@prettypunch.com

Threads and Flosses

Cotton embroidery floss is the mainstay of miniature punchneedle work. Both DMC and Anchor offer very high-quality floss in an extensive array of solid colors. Look for these at your local needlework or craft shop, or online.

Overdyed Cotton Embroidery Floss

The Gentle Art

www.thegentleart.com

Needle Necessities

www.needlenecessities.com/catalog/catalog.html

Weeks Dye Works

www.weeksdyeworks.com

Wool Thread

DMC

DMC Medicis and other wool-thread brands are available at needlework shops and online retailers.

French Wool Overdyed

www.needlenecessities.com/catalog/catalog.html

Renaiisance Dyeing

www.naturaldyeing.co.uk

Other Supplies

Fabric

Weaver's cloth can be found in nearly all fabric stores or online at www.woolenwhimsies.com.

Scissors

Snip-Eze from Havel's, Inc.

1-800-638-4770

www.havels.com

Embroidery Hoops

Susan Bates Hoop-La

These are available at many needlework and craft shops, as well as discount and online retailers.

Gripper Frame

www.woolenwhimsies.com

Fabric Pouch

www.lacis.com (Item LF27)

Wooden Box with Hinged Lid

Unpainted box available at Michaels
www.michaels.com

About the Author

Linda Repasky is a "pusher"—not of any illicit drugs or contraband, mind you, but of the amazing art form of punchneedle embroidery. She loves to watch people become entranced by using a tiny needle and thread to make rich, lush creations, and she knows that many of them will develop an addiction to this miniature form of needlework.

She hasn't always been this way. Before punching took over much of her life, she dabbled in a variety of arts and crafts. And then she found primitive rug hooking, which she adopted with a passion. Colorful strips of wool fabric took over her life. In short order, she became a "hooker."

It was only within the past few years that she stumbled across miniature punchneedle work. After teaching herself how to punch, she delved into learning all she could about this form of needlework and focused on perfecting her skills. Her miniature hooked rugs were so distinctive that they caught the attention of many and led her to develop courses where she could share this long-forgotten technique.

Linda lives in rural western Massachusetts, where she savors the quiet country life and continues to hook rugs and do punchneedle work. She finds the creativity and rhythm of hooking and punching to be a pleasant counterpoint to her full-time work as a manager in the federal government. She also designs and publishes patterns under the name *Woolen Whimsies* (www.woolenwhimsies.com) and teaches throughout New England. Linda has been recognized as one the country's top 200 artisans in *Early American Life* magazine's 2005 Directory of Traditional American Crafts. She welcomes readers' questions and comments via email at Linda@woolenwhimsies.com.

New and Bestselling Titles from

Martingale®
& COMPANY

America's Best-Loved Craft & Hobby Books®
America's Best-Loved Knitting Books®

America's Best-Loved Quilt Books®

NEW RELEASES

Alphabet Soup
Big Knitting
Big 'n Easy
Courtship Quilts
Crazy Eights
Creating Your Perfect Quilting Space
Crochet from the Heart
Fabulous Flowers
First Crochet
Fun and Funky Crochet
Joined at the Heart
Little Box of Knitted Ponchos and Wraps,
     The
Little Box of Knitted Throws, The
Merry Christmas Quilts
More Crocheted Aran Sweaters
Party Time!
Perfectly Brilliant Knits
Polka-Dot Kids' Quilts
Quilt Block Bonanza
Quilts from Grandmother's Garden
Raise the Roof
Saturday Sweaters
Save the Scraps
Seeing Stars
Sensational Knitted Socks
Sensational Sashiko
Strip-Pieced Quilts
Tea in the Garden
Treasury of Scrap Quilts, A

Our books are available
at bookstores and your
favorite craft, fabric,
and yarn retailers.
If you don't see
the title you're
looking for, visit us at
www.martingale-pub.com
or contact us at:

1-800-426-3126

International: 1-425-483-3313
Fax: 1-425-486-7596
Email: info@martingale-pub.com

APPLIQUÉ

Appliqué Takes Wing
Easy Appliqué Samplers
Garden Party
Stitch and Split Appliqué
Sunbonnet Sue: All through the Year
WOW! Wool-on-Wool Folk-Art Quilts

LEARNING TO QUILT

101 Fabulous Rotary-Cut Quilts
Happy Endings, Revised Edition
Loving Stitches, Revised Edition
Magic of Quiltmaking, The
Quilter's Quick Reference Guide, The
Sensational Settings, Revised Edition
Your First Quilt Book (or it should be!)

PAPER PIECING

40 Bright and Bold Paper-Pieced Blocks
50 Fabulous Paper-Pieced Stars
300 Paper-Pieced Quilt Blocks
Easy Machine Paper Piecing
Fanciful Quilts to Paper Piece
Hooked on Triangles
Quilter's Ark, A
Show Me How to Paper Piece

QUILTS FOR BABIES & CHILDREN

American Doll Quilts
Even More Quilts for Baby
More Quilts for Baby
Quilts for Baby
Sweet and Simple Baby Quilts

ROTARY CUTTING/SPEED PIECING

40 Fabulous Quick-Cut Quilts
365 Quilt Blocks a Year: Perpetual
     Calendar
1000 Great Quilt Blocks
Clever Quilts Encore
Endless Stars
Once More around the Block
Square Dance, Revised Edition
Stack a New Deck
Star-Studded Quilts
Strips and Strings

SCRAP QUILTS

More Nickel Quilts
Nickel Quilts
Scrap Frenzy
Successful Scrap Quilts

TOPICS IN QUILTMAKING

Basket Bonanza
Cottage-Style Quilts
Everyday Folk Art
Focus on Florals
Follow the Dots . . . to Dazzling Quilts
Log Cabin Quilts
More Biblical Quilt Blocks
Quilter's Home: Spring, The
Scatter Garden Quilts
Shortcut to Drunkard's Path, A
Strawberry Fair
Summertime Quilts
Tried and True
Warm Up to Wool

CRAFTS

Bag Boutique
Collage Cards
Creating with Paint
Painted Fabric Fun
Purely Primitive
Stamp in Color
Trashformations
Vintage Workshop, The: Gifts for All
     Occasions
Year of Cats...in Hats!, A

KNITTING & CROCHET

200 Knitted Blocks
365 Knitting Stitches a Year: Perpetual
     Calendar
Classic Crocheted Vests
Crocheted Socks!
Dazzling Knits
First Knits
Handknit Style
Knitted Throws and More for the Simply
     Beautiful Home
Knitting with Hand-Dyed Yarns
Little Box of Crocheted Hats and
     Scarves, The
Little Box of Scarves, The
Little Box of Scarves II, The
Little Box of Sweaters, The
Pleasures of Knitting, The
Pursenalities
Rainbow Knits for Kids
Sarah Dallas Knitting
Ultimate Knitted Tee, The